MAPS TO ECSTASY

"Gabrielle Roth is a unique and inspirational teacher, and this book is filled with her presence and her wisdom. I find Maps to Ecstasy fascinating, powerful, and delightful...."
—from the Foreword by Shakti Gawain
Author of *Creative Visualization*

"Gabrielle Roth is one of the most astounding beings alive and moving on the planet today. Her story and method move beyond ordinary definitions."
—Joan Halifax, Anthropologist
Author of *Shaman: The Wounded Healer*

"A wonderful and inspiring book that can lead people to a new level of understanding and give them the courage to follow their dreams."
—Lynn Andrews
Author of *Medicine Woman*

"Whether we live in urban or rural environments, our task is to remember and use the inherent instincts, rhythms, and intelligences available to us. Gabrielle Roth identifies these aspects of human nature and shows how we can apply perennial wisdom in contemporary times. Many books talk about shamanism; this one gives the reader an experience of shamanism."
—Angeles Arrien, Anthropologist

"Gabrielle Roth dances timeless wisdom to the rhythms of today and tomorrow. Maps to Ecstasy is a moving, inspiring and vivid experience from one of the world's greatest teachers . . . "
> —Brian Bates
> Author of The Way of Wyrd and
> The Way of the Actor

"Gabrielle Roth's book is a joy, a truly moving experience from a very fine teacher. It is both fun to read and immensely instructive. Don't expect to finish the book in a couple of sittings — keep it around and work with it over time like an old friend. 5 STARS FOR GABRIELLE ROTH AND MAPS TO ECSTASY!"
> —Brooke Medicine Eagle
> Native American Shaman

"You're in the desert. The raven comes down and talks to you in a dry, ancient voice. Don't mind the words — you recognize the voice. You knew it before you were born. That's Gabrielle."
> —Boris Grebenschikov
> Soviet Rock Musician

"Gabrielle Roth is a woman of power. In Maps to Ecstasy she takes us on a mythic journey through our lives and points the way to true balance. She challenges us to move and empowers us with the tools to dance our own dance."
> —Michael Toms
> Host/Producer of the U.S. radio series
> New Dimensions

"This book of impassioned, dancing wisdom teachings will delight you. As the saintly Mr. Gurdjieff might have said, Gabrielle Roth is a human being not in quotation marks."
> —Dr. Robert Masters, Director of Research
> The Foundation For Mind Research

MAPS TO ECSTASY

Teachings of an Urban Shaman

MAPS TO ECSTASY

Teachings of an Urban Shaman

GABRIELLE ROTH
WITH
JOHN LOUDON

FOREWORD BY SHAKTI GAWAIN

NATARAJ
PUBLISHING

Published by Nataraj Publishing
1561 S. Novato Blvd., Ste A
Novato, CA 94947

Cover design: Greg Wittrock
Text design: Nancy Benedict
Front cover photo: Robert Ansell
Back cover photo: Julie Skarratt
Illustration: Mark Reynolds
Typography: Walker Graphics

The author of this book does not dispense medical advice nor prescribe the use of any technique as a form of treatment for physical or mental problems without the advice of a physician either directly or indirectly. In the event you use any of the information in this book, neither the author nor the publisher can assume any responsibility for your actions. The intent of the author is only to offer information of a general nature to help you in your quest for personal growth.

First printing, April 1989
Printed in the U.S.A.
on acid-free recycled paper.

Dedicated to Robert and Jonathan

CONTENTS

FOREWORD

Like Gabrielle Roth, my initial opening to God, to the Universe, to bliss, came through dance. My first real experience of surrendering to a force greater than myself happened as I surrendered my body to the ecstatic experience of dancing freely and spontaneously, from an energy that flowed from deep within me. That was many years ago, and I continue to follow the dancing path, returning over and over again to my body—its natural energy, feelings, movement—as the surest guide to living each moment deeply and truthfully.

When I met Gabrielle a few years ago, I immediately recognized her as a sister soul. I was drawn to experiencing her work, and loved the trance-like spell she created in her workshops, allowing the participants to contact and express deeper and deeper layers of themselves. She has since become a good friend, so it is with pleasure that I introduce her book to you. Gabrielle Roth is a unique and inspirational teacher, and this book is filled with her presence and her wisdom. I find *Maps to Ecstasy* fascinating, powerful, and delightful, and I have a feeling you will, too.

Shakti Gawain

ACKNOWLEDGMENTS

I guess it would be easy to write acknowledgments if I only owed a little to a few people, but my life and work have been touched so deeply by so many. In general, I have received something from everyone I've ever worked with. My most important teachers have been my students. I can only lead by following and they have always taken me exactly where I needed to go.

I am deeply indebted to my whole family. Especially to my father, for initiating me into the art of living and of dying. To my mother, for her constant flow of unconditional love and support. To my husband, Rob, there are no words to convey how profoundly he has served the development of my work in general and this book in particular. I thank him for being my best friend, wisest teacher, and constant collaborator—the one who dances with me through all the changes. And to my son, Jonathan, for being my deepest pipeline to my real self. I am honored to be his mom, and often humbled by his wisdom, some of which has made it to the pages of this book.

I am also indebted to Oscar Ichazo—for teaching me how to tell the difference between who I am and who I am not. I could not have written Chapters Three and Four of this book without his teachings.

My deepest thanks to the "Mirrors," kindred spirits with whom I worked and performed daily for three years, and whose courage, honesty, and commitment in stripping down their psyches and performing their pain enabled me to develop the material in Chapter Four. These warriors of Ritual Theater gave life to a whole new level of my work. Thank you. Jay and Amber Kaplan, Martha Clark Peabody, Elliot Sobel, Melissa Rosenberg, Robert Ansell, Ma Prem Lolita, Nirvesha, Bonita Mugnani, and Bobby Miller.

I must also express my appreciation to the musical component of the Mirrors, a group of gifted musical artists who, over the years, helped me to develop the musical landscape of my journey, thereby deepening my understanding of where I was going and how to get there. Thank you. Dolores Holmes, Otto Richter, Jeffrey Hoffman, Wendy Schubart, Eric Silverman, Joyce Leigh Bowden, Tim Boyce, Serpentine, Tim Scott, Bebop Brown, Gene Heimlich, and most especially, Raphael, Robert Ansell, and Gordie Ryan.

Along the way I have received unconditional support from Michael Murphy, Dick Price, and Nancy Lunney, who provided me with a laboratory at Esalen Institute in which my entire body of work was developed. And my heartfelt thanks to Kathryn Altman, who has continuously blessed me with her support, love, home, car, and closet. She has been instrumental in helping me move my work into the world, as have Eric Iverson and Roger Housden.

My special thanks to two extraordinary modern shamans, Jack Schwarz, for illuminating my vision again and again, and inspiring me to keep on keeping on, and to Boris Grebenschikov, for sharing his creative process with me, thereby profoundly inspiring my own.

My deepest struggle has been to bring my work to the written page, to freeze in time something that is essentially moving. This could not have been done without the wisdom and sensitivity of my collaborator, John Loudon. His faith in me and this project was as important as his enormous talent in bringing this book to fruition.

I deeply appreciate my publisher, New World Library. Shakti Gawain has been a good friend and formidable ally;

Shamans transmit to their people in sign, song, and dance the nature of the cosmic geography that has been revealed to them in the process of initiation trances and soul journeys. Map-makers and myth-dancers, shamans live internally in a multi-dimensional realm continuous with so-called ordinary reality.

Joan Halifax[1]

PROLOGUE

Invitation to the Dance of Life

I went to church, but God wasn't there;
I said everybody's prayers
Till something deep inside me cried,
"I need the beat to be satisfied."
I got off my knees and on my feet
Took my rock 'n' roll prayers back on the street.
I gotta dance,
Gotta dance.

Gabrielle Roth[2]

I was raised on rock 'n' roll, fast food, and subways. I've never been on any trips to exotic cultures, or studied tribal techniques. I read the papers, go to the movies, worry about what to fix for dinner, and go to work like most people. Only for me, going to work is going on a journey—a journey to an ecstatic level of consciousness.

This book is a map to ecstasy in all its forms. Ecstasy is my high, a natural state of pure being. Ecstasy is my experience of god. It is a state of total aliveness and unity, unity of body, heart, mind, soul and spirit. It is what we need to heal our psychic dismemberment. We can't go there divided, body against mind, mind against heart, or any other way. I know the pain of dismemberment, of being divided against and from myself. Ecstasy has been my healing.

I was born to move, and to teach others to move. To move their bodies. And their hearts. Their minds. Their souls. Their spirits. Healing the rift between their dream and their reality, their experience and their potential.

My work is a marriage of art and healing, meant to catalyze our wholeness through dance, song, poetry, ritual, and meditation. I've learned through suffering and experimenting how to transform daily life into sacred art.

From an early age, my energies were those of a healer: I easily slipped into trance, could see through bodies, smell death, feel birth, know when someone was in pain and how to guide them through it. It's always been instinctive for me to turn suffering into art. I call it survival art.

My work is to empower people through the creative process. I expect that others are just like me: they want to wake up; they want to be set free. Freeing the body to experience the power of being. Expressing the heart to experience the power of loving. Emptying the mind to experience the power of self-knowledge. Awakening the soul to experience the power of seeing. Embodying the spirit to experience the power of healing.

Movement is my medicine. Rhythm is our universal mother tongue. It's the language of the soul. But it's a forgotten language because we live mostly cut off from our soul, the source of real personal power. We live in our heads. We live some idea of who we are. We think that all we are is our personality. But a body without soul has no rhythm. A person without moves is a walking stiff.

In my vision, everybody is a dancer. Everybody has a shaman inside. Waiting for a wake-up call. Ready for dancing on the edge.

Shamanic healing is a journey. It involves stepping out of our habitual roles, our conventional scripts, and improvising a dancing path. The dancing path leads us from the inertia of sleepwalking to the ecstasy of living the spirit of the moment. Too often our lives automatically get channeled into narrow, secure patterns, set into deadly routines. Some of us want out. Some of us want to let go and wake up to the power buried within us.

To do this, we have to live on the edge, between the lines, somewhere between matter and spirit, masculine and feminine, darkness and light, leader and follower, stillness and motion. We venture like tightrope walkers over the abyss of the unknown. I like it on the edge. I take others with me. This is my work; it is a journey from the ghetto of the ego to the expanses of the full self, a level of awareness that floods everyday life with vital energy.

This book offers choreography for dancing on the edge—not the set steps of classical dance, but guidelines for expressive creativity. It is a guidebook of self-exploration, affording topical maps for each reader to chart. The aim is to get moving. To awaken the shamanic dimension of ourselves. To unleash the body, heart, mind, soul, spirit to discover the dancer, singer, poet, actor, healer within. This is an ecstatic experience.

I live for this experience. I've spent my life making maps that lead to it on all levels of being. It is a Silver Desert—an illuminative, visionary level of consciousness.

The first time I glimpsed the Silver Desert, I was nine years old. Eva took me there. She was my first spiritual teacher, though of course I didn't realize it until long after. I was living with my parents near Golden Gate Park in San Francisco.

I'm playing with some friends in the street. We're throwing ourselves recklessly into a large hedge on the

side of a house. Suddenly an elderly woman bolts out
of the house and scares away my friends. I stay, as my
friends run off, mesmerized by her energy and captivated
by her strangely gentle scolding, "Children, can't you
hear the leaves and branches screaming? Don't you know
they're in pain?"

She invites me in for tea. Her eyes are blue tunnels,
her hair silver. Her body is taut, slender, and her conversation is punctuated with a quick, high-pitched laugh.
The house is flooded with music and the smells of soup
cooking. Enchanted, I know I have found not just a new
friend, but a friend for a new part of myself.

We spend endless afternoons drinking tea and talking. I don't even know that I'm learning more here than
at school, because it's all so effortless.

But it's in dying that Eva teaches me the most.

I have a vision of her death during morning Mass. I
go every day. I love the solitude, the stillness of the old
Catholic church. Just me and a bunch of old ladies in
black, rocking and rolling our rosary beads. This particular morning, as the priest serves Holy Communion, I
see something moving above his head. It looks like an
eagle. It looks like Eva. She's a see-through shadow of
herself, laughing so loud I'm sure the priest can hear. He
doesn't bat an eye, has no idea what's going on, and
that's when I know she's dying. She blows me a kiss as I
fight back my tears.

I'm terrified. I don't even go to school. I run to her
house where I find her very much alive. I tell her what
I've seen, and she speaks to me in that always surprising
way of hers. She convinces me that death is not negative.
I can't focus on her words, make any logical sense of
them. All I get is that death seems like an exotic recipe,
a wonderful way to make a pie.

Her energy begins to shift inward. Our visits are
shot through with silence. Or music. Sometimes Cho-

pin. Sometimes Frank Sinatra. Sometimes a wailing gypsy.

Eva gradually moves into the bedroom. It's a permanent move. "She's moving in, and out," I think. One afternoon, while reading to her, the color of the room begins to change. It slowly becomes bathed in silver. I see a thread of her silver hair extend right out of her head and turn into a thread of light that penetrates deep inside me. I bask in a silver glow, a meditation without effort, an ecstatic tranquility. I feel like I've floated to another level, been transported to another place. I think I'm in heaven.

Eva is dead. Her spirit is gone. I close her eyes the way she told me to. And I keep reading to her. I don't want to leave. When I do, I close the door and don't look back. She told me not to.

Eva's death was a beginning for me, an initiation into a fresh way of seeing life and death, a way of dissolving, at least momentarily, the boundaries between body and soul, now and forever. It was my first encounter with ecstasy.

I found the Silver Desert as a child, but like most people, I lost it as I grew up. Our culture does not value or even believe in ecstasy. All too soon the soul starves.

Our bodies get locked into patterns. We get stiff with repetition. Our hearts also become rigidified into automatic routines. We're soon numb, insensitive to what we really feel. And our minds are quickly blinded by unquestioned assumptions, guiding attitudes that don't allow us to see what's out there, let alone explore the world's fullness. We're programmed for boredom.

Long before I suspected it, my involvement with dance was my way of countering these inertial tendencies with energy, with movement. Right from the start, I discovered that when I dance I bypass my personality. It can't keep up. It has no sense of rhythm, because it's like a robot, programmed to only certain patterns of movement. When I dance, I break free. I make up my own steps, let the beat all the way into my soul. I ride on the waves of music like a surfer. I bump against parts of myself, go between, around, stretch what I know. I go where I've never been. Through dance I've journeyed through my body into my heart, past my mind into another dimension of existence, a dimension I call ecstasy, total communion with the spirit.

Moving with the spirit has taught me all I know. And all I know is that ecstatic movement is empowering and healing. My method, my shamanic madness, comes not from books, but from living and dancing. My laboratory has been the auditorium, the studio, the dance floor, the theater, the streets. It's been a long initiation.

In my teens, I fell into anorexia, taking the body/spirit split to the edge. My crisis came from the feeling that I had to choose, choose between heaven and hell. My body was hell, struggling with the passion of my emerging sexuality. The "high" I got from starving myself was heavenly. I went for the spirit. I lived on the edge of life and death, of self-hatred and vague longing. When I finally broke out of this pattern of self-destruction, it was a radical decision to choose life, even while dancing on the edge.

At the beginning of my journey, teachers came to me in all forms. My initiation began on playgrounds and senior-citizen centers. To work my way through college, I taught dance and drama to kids and old people for a variety of recreation departments. At least that's what I thought I was doing. They were my first Zen masters. They taught me to lead by following. It was impossible to "control" 300 kids on a playground or 50 seniors, each with their own worlds and fixed ideas. It was impossible to impose my great plans—plans I may have stayed up half the night creating—unless they happened (as they occasionally did) to fit into their flow. More often than not, to retain my sanity, I had to drop my brilliant ideas and flow, spontaneously creating movement and dance out of the energy in the room or on the playground. I had to draw them out from where they were. I followed them into the moment, and found it a magical place.

It was there I first discovered the rhythms by which energy flows, by paying attention to their moves, the sudden gear shifts in intensity and style. The kids especially changed very quickly, and I had to shift with them: one minute I'd be telling stories, the next moment creating a new tag game; then I'd be explaining why two dogs were stuck together; soon I'd be umpiring a baseball game; and then a crying kid would need consoling. I had a day-after-day intensive in improvisation, intuiting just what to do in the moment, creating something special out of just a hint, an accident, a confrontation. But mostly the children and the seniors, each in their own way, inspired me just to be myself. And looking back, I realize that my real job was to keep their energy channeled in positive, creative directions.

I'm hired to teach patients at Agnew State Hospital how to dance. My whole class is made up of schizophrenics. Here I am with a room full of 25 or 30 people, each in his or her own reality. One guy is umpiring his own baseball game. Another is doing the hula. Another is directing imaginary traffic.

How can I teach these people to dance? What steps can I offer that they can imitate? No one is home in their bodies. Barely breathing, their limbs limp, their eyes vacant, except for spasms of activity, they're slumping sacks of flesh.

The answer comes as soon as I surrender to the fact that I really can't teach them to "dance." All I can do to serve them is seduce them into moving, to put their realities into motion. They can make up their own steps.

I enter their worlds and begin to choreograph their fantasies. We all move around the bases, swing invisible bats, do the hula, direct emergency traffic. Eventually,

they all get moving, acting out each other's trips, and I
just ride the waves of their energy as well as I can.

I was straddling two worlds. On the one hand I was
primarily occupied with going to college: getting all my
creative impulses educated out of me, feeling completely
out of place, studying subjects I didn't give a damn about.
And on the other hand, to support myself, I was working
with kids, seniors, the mentally disturbed, and that was
keeping my spirit alive. They were teaching me how to be
open, responsive. I listened to their stories, felt their pain,
saw their psychic wounds, and did my best to be there for
them. And it was with them that my education really took
place.

I started breaking loose from my cultural bonds, learning the connections between the body, the heart, and the
mind when I went to Europe and lived there for three years
after graduating from college. When I arrived, I barely spoke
any of the languages; I'd just mastered the bare linguistic
necessities to get by, all in the present tense. I began to feel
like a free spirit, no longer bound by the presumptions and
expectations I'd grown up with. The past didn't exist. I
couldn't speak in the past tense, and had no past with the
people I was meeting. I could make myself up from scratch
every minute. For the first time in my life, I was nobody's
daughter or friend or student or teacher. I was alone, just
me, and it was exhilarating; I had a taste of what it was
like to be truly free to be myself.

In Europe, art became my obsession. I lived in mu-
seums, consuming art whole, absorbing each painting and
sculpture in search of maps to my soul. I got a job as an art
model—no language necessary.

Sitting inert in the middle of high-ceilinged rooms
with stone walls, I let my image be captured, constantly
redefined from myriad perspectives. After each session,
I wander through the room taking in hundreds of visions

of my body, of my self. Some catch me in soft shimmering pastels, others in bold oil strokes. Some see me as a collage, others as a flowing line. For some I'm a bird in flight or a wounded fawn, for others an ancient Egyptian cat or a lithe tigress. Beautiful, ugly, bad, good. Some I like; some I don't. They're all me; yet none are me.

Being a model, I learn subconsciously to be detached from all my own flickering self-images. I see that they can all be true, but none are permanent. And I'm amazed to find that this realization doesn't plunge me into nihilistic despair. Instead, I feel a fresh surge of a force stronger than all those smaller images of myself. Fleetingly, I run into my soul.

I began to see more clearly that art is not just ornamental, an enhancement of life, but a path in itself, a way out of the predictable and conventional, a map to self-discovery. Still, it was just intuition until I could *live* it, use it.

I'd studied dance most of my life before I went to Europe. My training was very traditional, all involved with form. My dance depended on mirrors, techniques, turn-out, bloody toes. Starving my body and conforming to the one way things had to be done.

Dance meant imitation, whether the form was ballet, modern, or James Brown funk. The focus was always on someone else's steps. It became more and more difficult to feel good about dancing as dancing became more and more tied to right and wrong. It was "right" to move my arm to a certain height in a certain shape and "wrong" to let it go where it wanted to go. I left so many classes in despair, judging myself adversely for not being Martha Graham. Somehow, dance classes just kept proving to me that I wasn't good enough.

And, all the time, the clock was running. The conventional wisdom was that I could dance until I was thirty—after that, I would be over the hill, washed up.

Europe began to change it all for me. In Spain, my fledgling spirit really spread its wings and began to fly. A new dance was born. Once more, I was suddenly transported to the Silver Desert. I was initiated by two women, neither of whom said a word but conveyed everything I needed to know through their spirit-filled bodies:

In the small town of Sitges, I am walking along the old avenidas with alcoves that are Spain's secret treasures—narrow walkways that open on to recessed terraces, gardens, plazas. Then from one nondescript archway I hear the sound of an unseen guitar strumming. I'm drawn, and enter the inner sanctum.

In the shaded privacy of the garden, an ancient man sits on a low wall playing his guitar. His eyes are closed. An old woman stands beside him, with eyes closed as well. Slowly she begins to dance, focused on her own movement, yet dancing with the music as with a partner. Her dancing uplifts me. In a moment, all my concerns about age and time and the rules of dance are swept away.

In her dance I see that the body is the wife of the spirit. Age doesn't diminish that vital marriage; it only deepens it. Male and female, music and movement, body and spirit—a liquid harmony, more potent with age. Dance, the art of moving which puts us dynamically together.

That evening I go to a club to see a real gypsy dancer. Sitting in the sultry air, I smell jasmine so strongly I can taste it. I nurse a Singapore Sling and stare at the bare wooden stage.

La Chunga bursts onto the stage with the first strum of the guitar. She is total. She is raw passion, unbridled power. She has crystal ball eyes and the posture of a statue that has been standing at the gates of the Mediterranean for a thousand years. She is a many-faceted jewel, flashing multiple depths. She is a total presence, a bolt from beyond, commanding the unadorned proscenium with bare feet and bare soul.

La Chunga rips me open. Her trance is electric. It fires me with ecstasy. Her overflowing energy releases me to dance with abandon. She burns away my guilt-ridden, diminished, negative, ambivalent persona, the wimpy role-player I so readily become. She stamps out my "original sin" with her blazing feet, and I'm whisked away to the Silver Desert, drenched in the blood-red glow of a Mediterranean sunset. I'm thrilled and terrified to know the power of unleashed passion, and there's no turning back.

La Chunga was a shotgun that blasted through my carefully constructed personality and let my soul pour out into real time. Spain was Holy Communion for my hungry spirit.

Though I never spoke with La Chunga, I had a dream about her that sealed her message to me: I had watched her dance and fought through crowds to find her afterwards. Breathless, I stumbled upon her leaning against a tree with her hands folded simply behind her. "La Chunga," I said (in the dream I could speak Spanish), "I want so to dance like you." She waved away my plea with the retort, "Then, dance like you, fool!"

The permission to dance with passion and to dance forever jolted me from unconscious inertia and self-conscious imitation to the intuitive dance of my soul. In this dance nobody knew the steps, not even me. As soon as I committed myself to simply moving, letting the inside flow out, I eliminated the need to live up to forms, to expectations created by someone else. I entered the realm of ecstatic dance.

Ecstatic dance became my way of jumping out of my personality into my soul. Whenever I got stuck in my head, I did whatever it took to get dancing, to escape the safe, boring confines of being reasonable. I had no idea that I would spend my life taking others with me.

In the mid-sixties, I returned from Europe to the States to teach American history and drama to high school students. The country was tense with race riots, sit-ins, demonstrations. After Martin Luther King, Jr.'s tragic assassination, a large contingent of the school's black students marched en masse, in silence, through the school. Their somber ritual shook up most of the white kids in the school as well as the administration. My junior and senior students, mostly white, looked to me as an adult who'd seen a lot of the world and begged me to teach them black history, teach them what was going on. They wanted to understand.

But could I teach them? I remembered so many black and white stories that my heart ached. I had a lot of black friends. But I'd never been black. I only knew the shame of being white. How was I to teach black history?

I moved on instinct:

> For six weeks we go over current events, the history of slavery in the United States, segregation, the entrenched causes of racial violence and revolutionary outbreaks such as the Watts riots. Painfully, honestly, we air our personal prejudices, searching for the sources of our own ingrained attitudes. I also give them a programmed text about blacks in America put out by the Behavioral Research Lab. It includes historical facts about blacks, social statistics and leads to a true/false test. I tell them that anybody, even someone who'd never been to school, could pass the test, and that as a favor to them I'd base their whole grade (and the seniors needed to pass to graduate) on the test.
>
> When exam day comes, I don't give them the Behavioral Research Lab test. Instead, I give them the "Chitlin Test" with questions like, "1) How long do you boil

chitlins to get them tender? 2) How much is the welfare check in this state for a woman with one dependent?" The test had been prepared by a group of black educators who were upset that most standardized tests were so biased toward a white social environment. I'll never forget Howard Schwartz's reaction. He'd been getting straight A's since kindergarten. His was the first hand to shoot up, the first voice of protest. "But, Miss Roth, this material isn't related to the text or the syllabus for this course." He was in a state of panic. I cut him short. "Howard, I'm sure you're an expert on black history. Just sit down and finish your test." He couldn't believe this was happening to him, his perfect record being besmirched by this off-the-wall test.

Only 3 out of about 175 kids pass the test. For two days, they are miserable, depressed, angry. They feel violated, betrayed, and think that they won't be able to go on to college. Then on the third day, I walk in, amazed that they still trust me enough not to have complained to their parents and the administration. Why did I do this to them? How could I be so unfair? How could I promise an easy test based on the text and then spring this surprise on them? I look out over each class and say, "Well, you wanted me to teach you black history. Tell me: How does it feel to be a 'nigger'?"

Their patterns of perception are shaken. They start to look at the world afresh, from a new perspective. What more important lesson in black history could I teach them than the *experience* of injustice?

The next day I give them the right test.

I was walking on edges, risking disaster, working below the surface, using drama, shock, humor, anything I could drum up to create movement and change. I didn't know what the hell I was doing, but whatever it was, I had to do it. I was learning my trade, but nobody—least of all me—

knew what it was. That's why I kept losing my way and then finding the path again.

I eventually gave up teaching because all I really wanted to do was dance—even if it didn't pay my rent. I had to take that risk. Now, instead of taking three classes a week I was taking three classes a day. By day, I surrendered to the demands of form. By night, I abandoned myself to the passion of ecstatic dance. It never dawned on me that I might be able to perform or teach this form of formless dance. The only choice I felt was available to me was to become a professional dancer. God had other plans. My knee began mysteriously collapsing. An old ski injury rerouted me from "performing" to "teaching." The doctors said I would never dance again. It looked like I'd have to spend the rest of my life in a body that couldn't dance. The ultimate blow.

My ensuing depression led me to Big Sur to take sensitivity training. But the leader of the group was so insensitive that I dropped out and went down to the baths. In giving up, I found what I was looking for.

It's my first venture into the infamous baths at Esalen Institute. I'm nervous about being nude. I feel self-conscious and awkward, as my arched bare feet make their way down the stone steps. I turn the corner and blunder right in on an old man who looks like Santa Claus, balling, as he'd put it, a lady's brains out right in the hot tub. I clutch my towel, dash back up the hill, and hide out in my room, chain-smoking until dinner.

The old man sits at my table. He upbraids some lady for asking him to pass the salt. Suddenly, he turns on me and says in a heavy German accent, "What 'ave we here, a movie star?" I glare right back at him and don't miss a beat, "No, I'm a filmmaker. My specialty is hot-tub sex featuring horny old men." No response. We hold the stare until he bursts into laughter.

I had no idea that I had just met Fritz Perls, the father of Gestalt Therapy. Fritz, it turned out, loved dancers. He was fascinated by the fact that I had taught dance to kids on playgrounds, old folks in senior citizen homes, schizophrenics in mental wards, junkies in halfway houses. At the time, I just thought of them as odd jobs I'd done to put myself through college. But he saw how working with these people demanded living in the moment, and that's what he cared about.

In his work he uprooted therapy from the past and planted it in the now. Early traumas, recurrent dreams, past relationships, hurts, anger—he had people make everything present tense. Whatever's happening, it's happening now. The past is now; the future is now. Live it.

And he recognized the same character in me. I had never thought of my work as healing or therapeutic, but Fritz was quick to make the association. He promptly invited me to teach movement to his Gestalt Therapy group. I had never had such stage fright; I couldn't dance, and here I was supposed to teach it, but I went ahead anyway.

> I arrive with fifty records, three sticks of incense, and at least ten plans. There are bodies all over the room, sitting, standing, leaning against the wall, talking, or watching me guardedly.
>
> I dash over to the stereo, feeling as self-conscious as a pubescent ballerina. The stereo's broken. Panic. There go all my plans. I feel the motley throng staring at my back, daring me to get them to move.
>
> Desperate, I whirl around to eye my enemy. And then I pick up on this mantra pounding in my brain, "Just dance, just dance!"
>
> So I just start to move and the words come out, "OK, just lie down and let your whole body sink into the floor. Open your legs, relax your hands, release your jaw. Feel

your breath, ride it like a surfer rides a wave deep into the center of yourself. Now, just move your right hand.... Good, now your left hand.... Open and close both hands.... Open and close your mouth ... your hands ... your legs.... Close up into a ball.... Open.... Close.... Now with partners...."

I move us through the parts of the body. Follow the body like a map into a deeper sense of self.

A new level of my work had begun. I became the movement specialist in residence at Esalen. It was the sixties, anything was possible. There was a revolution going on, and here I was in the middle of it.

I'm on the deck at Esalen. It's night. I've been watching others dance and seducing people to move for months, all the time afraid to really dance myself. Memories of doctors talking about bone pins and knee operations haunt me.

Under a full moon, the mountains fall into the sea. The deck is crowded with bodies, some hip, some straight, all watching the Big Sur drummers set up for a jam session.

The air is electric as they begin to play. Suddenly, they click, and the beat begins to pound in my body, shattering my inertia. I'm drawn from the shadows—everything is calling me to the dance.

All of my fear disappears in the throbbing pulse of the drums. I forget my knee. I forget that I can't dance. Nothing can stop my spirit from moving, not even my body. I let go as I'm swept away in a vortex of motion to the deepest level of ecstatic trance I've ever experienced. I break through to the spirit of the dance as I leave all form behind—forever. My dance and I are one. It is my dance—my body is flying. I am a raven, carrying the sorrow of children on my ebony wings, a wolf, howling

on the edge of the night. My shape keeps shifting and
I follow it to the Silver Desert.

It was a moment of great truth for me when I found that
I could move even though I couldn't "dance," oddly enough,
the very thing I had been teaching others for years. I had
been on a journey to the land of the spirit and was reborn.
My healing crisis ended in my ecstatic trance. And the
ecstasy I found was what everyone was looking for. I became obsessed with mapping my journey there and back
so I could take others with me.

Fritz was the only person I could talk to about all this.
He and I became good friends. One day he came upon me
reading his book, *In and Out of the Garbage Pail*. He tore
it out of my hands and threw it over the ridge behind us
into the Pacific and shouted, "I wrote this because I couldn't
dance." Not long after that, I caught Fritz in the throes of
shaking up someone's self-conceptions—gesticulating
wildly, screwing up his face into a dozen masks, each a
full-blown character. I said, "Hey Fritz, who says you can't
dance?"

Overall, Fritz gave me a simple message: "I see who
you are. I see what you do. Do it."

For the next three years Esalen was an intense laboratory for the development of my work. And in my lab I had a
constant flow of bodies passing through: would-be models
chiseled into blue jeans, gurus of the day, egos caught in
tangles of gold chains, faces fresh from the pages of *Life*
magazine. I saw the privileged, the envied, the with-it,
have-it-all set. Doctors, lawyers, psychiatrists, movie stars—
all uptight, all in pain. Here they were, the captors of the
American Dream all standing in line, waiting to scream,
to pound their way out of their air-conditioned nightmare.

Once I took their words away, whatever they had "all
together" started to fall apart. They didn't know how to
hold it together or how to let it all come crashing down.

They couldn't catch the beat of the music or feel the beat of their hearts. They couldn't look each other in the eye or let themselves cry. Hooked on speed and image, they couldn't just be here when there was nowhere to go, nothing to show.

I danced my pain in these movement sessions and let everybody else dance theirs, whatever it was. Crack the ice, melt the mask, feel something in your bones. Get down. Come alive.

And the bodies spoke to me. I saw stories in flesh, the untold tales of dead arms just hanging there, of pelvises locked in "Park," of clenched fists and locked jaws, in physiques molded into attitudes of "I'm not good enough" or "Get out of my way." Chests sunk in shame, shoulders riding high, voices edgy with anger or constricted with fear. The body never lies.

The All-American people show paraded by every day. Nice. Normal. Neutral. Neurotic. Every body, even famous bodies, desperately wanted to be somebody and didn't have a clue as to how. Who could believe that the secret lay in movement? In making a home of this flesh we cart around like a burden?

I came to see that we were all suffering from "trizophrenia": thinking one thing, feeling another, acting out a third. How often I would think "yes," feel "no," and hear myself say, "I'll get back to you." Or I'd feel pissed off, think "I'm wrong," and act polite. Or I'd think "I'm cool," feel insecure, and act tough. Trizophrenia is enervating. You're drained, powerless; there's no energy center. You feel dismembered, a jumble of parts, just reacting to whatever comes at you. Everybody in my sessions knew the feeling.

But for reasons I hardly knew, moving started pulling them together, gave them a sense of a center, kindled a spark of spirit. Every day I was discovering that if you just set people in motion, they'll heal themselves. And I started finding shortcuts for them on the journey back to wholeness.

Still, I had no name for what I was doing. No language. People in my workshops were changing, bursting out of their straitjacket personalities and battering down the walls of their defense systems. I'd chanced on a way to unleash the spirit, but I had no structure, no method, no system. In fact, I had no ideas at all, just instincts.

I was still insecure enough that the formlessness of my vocation disturbed me. When people on airplanes and at parties asked me, "What do you do?", I'd have to improvise some answer each time, but I always felt ridiculous and evasive. What was I supposed to say, "I unleash ecstasy"?

I had yet to put all my parts together, to own my power, to find my voice.

It was around this time that people began describing my work as shamanic. I had to look it up in the dictionary, and that didn't help: "Shaman: a medicine man [not woman]; one acting as both priest and doctor who works with the supernatural." Super natural. What's more natural than natural? I rejected the whole idea.

But who was I? How could I make sense of what I was doing? Was I for real, or was I a fraud? I needed my own teacher. And when some friends of mine returned from Chile visibly transformed and exuding enthusiasm for the teachings of Oscar Ichazo, I immediately sensed that this was the teacher I was looking for.

It turned out that Ichazo was moving to New York, and very quickly I found myself at the Essex Hotel where he was conducting his Arica training in spiritual development. Oscar Ichazo, a black Bolivian cat with laser eyes, had broken the code. A master teacher, a shapeshifter, a shamanic superman, he lived in satori and beckoned students to join him there, if they dared. I took the plunge. He asked me, "Who are you? Where are you going? How will you get there?" I evaded, I floundered, I wavered. I flunked the entrance exam. And that was the first step.

Oscar showed me a map to my psyche: how it had been formed and wounded. My wound was blatant—a totally negative self-image. I didn't know who I was or how to be with myself. I kept myself busy at all times, filling in the black hole inside me. That's why the first exercise, the "Desert Experience," terrified me.

> I'm in a hotel room in Manhattan. Everything in the room is draped with white sheets. The phone, the radio, the TV are all turned off. The blinds are pulled, mirrors covered. No distractions. Just me. Nothing to do, no one to talk to, nothing to smoke, hardly anything to eat or drink—just a few figs and some apple juice. For three days.

> I've finally been asked to hand in all my scripts, been stripped of all my facades. No faces to put on. Nobody to be somebody for.

> At first, I panic. I'm so used to running from one excitement to another, to being busy about outside things, that the solitude I claim to treasure feels like emptiness, life at zero. And, of course, that's what it is. I'm so accustomed to being in flight, that I collapse like an origami bird.

> The first day I fall into an exhausted heap and sleep. I wake up in the middle of the night, but there's nothing to do but to surrender to being here. I begin to let go and relax, settle into myself like a lounging cat. Nobody to please. Nothing to perform. Nowhere to go. Just be here now.

> Slowly the silence, the void, begins to envelop me, as nurturing as a womb. A different sort of fullness— deep, personal, unlike the filled days of demands, distractions, evasions—begins to emerge.

> Solitary confinement in an urban desert. I realize that I'd forgotten how to stop, how to be still. So I've

lost touch with the Silver Desert. For now, though, just being here is enough.

On the third night, Oscar comes to teach me an exercise he calls "Trespasso." We each sit in a full lotus position with a candle between us and look into each other's left eye. He instructs me to relax, feel my breath, empty my mind, and silently repeat the mantra, "We are one," over and over till it dissolves into my breath.

My mantra fades into his motionless body. His face melts into intense distortions, like exploding voodoo masks. He appears as a Buddha. The room turns red, then gold. He disappears. I can see the wall behind him, yet still hear him breathe. I drop my mind and fall into the void.

Gradually he comes back into focus. We chant "OM" and bow deeply, honoring each other's spirit. He blows out the candle and leaves me in the dark. But I'm aglow. Fresh winds from nowhere blow through me that night. I brim with my own power, the power of simply being who I am.

All at once, it's time to leave, and I don't want to go. I stay till the last moment. The maid needs to clean the room. She's losing patience. I walk out to the elevator, but I can't get my finger to press the "Down" button. How long will this bliss last? Will I make it through the lobby, out to the street, into next week? But I remember a passage from the I Ching: "We cannot lose what really belongs to us, even if we throw it away."

Over the next three years, with Oscar's guidance, I discovered the complex mechanisms that create our personalities, our daily patterns of thinking and acting in the world. I learned to recognize my own patterns inside and out. I began to maintain some distance from my ego—that false sense of self, the constructed persona that we think we really are—and to find my *true* self, to live at zero. Being fully present here and now, not living in the past or the future or freighting every experience with emotional baggage.

It was my ego, I learned, that was causing all my pain. It was full of constant chatter, judgment, denial, hopelessness, excesses, fixed beliefs, the need to control things. I was unable to really move, to breathe, to explore. Egos don't dance. They never make it to the Silver Desert. Our egos are menageries of dull, predictable soap opera characters we learn to play. They keep us from being who we are, knowing how to live and what to do, by sapping our creative power and sabotaging the authentic expressions of human energy—the dancer, the singer, the poet, the actor, the healer.

After three years of studying and teaching Arica work I decided I needed to dance again.

I meet another Latin livewire, Alejandro Jodorowsky, the brilliant filmmaker who made "El Topo." He jolts me into a level of power and movement beyond any I had yet experienced. The first thing he says to me is, "I hear you are an artist. You change people's lives. Tell me what you are doing now." He catches me completely by surprise. I stammer something about teaching Arica work for Oscar.

"Oh," he says with a mysterious smile, and he begins to move. His eyes hold mine, and I begin to follow. We become a stream of motion, like tai chi partners in a trance.

Abruptly, he snaps his fingers, "Can Oscar dance like you?" "No," I say meekly. "Then, why don't you teach him?" He sees right through me. He sees my panic. Oscar is like a god to me. I can't imagine that I can teach him anything.

The next day, Alejandro and I sit facing each other in straight-backed chairs about 25 feet apart in a living room filled with Eastern art, Afghani rugs, Moroccan pillows. He looks gorgeous, and frightening: black leather pants, purple silk shirt, gleaming black boots, square, burnished face, thick silver-black hair, penetrating black eyes. He glares. "Gabrielle, do me a big favor." I nod. "Cut your father's balls off!" Calmly, he stands up and leaves the room. I don't understand. I love my daddy. He is good. He is always there.

It was only with time that I saw he wasn't talking about my father, but about my tendency to habitually elevate men and diminish myself. Oscar was not the only man I made into a god. But I was beginning to learn to beware hero-worshiping, especially when the hero is a teacher. The ego's traps are hard to escape, for everyone.

After meeting Jodorowsky, I went back to Big Sur to teach movement again. Essentially, the work was the same, but I was different. More of me was available. I'd learned to be present, to be still.

This time around Gregory Bateson, the noted anthropologist, was there. He had become Esalen's community sage. He was dying of cancer, and he was doing it openly, bravely, gracefully. He participated in several of my ritual theater labs, and we even co-led a workshop we called "The Shaman and the Anthropologist," his last appearance as a teacher.

Gregory was one of the most inspired and inspiring individuals I ever knew. Many powerful teachers had appreciated my work and recommended it to their students, but Gregory actually did it. He surrendered himself to it totally. Seventy-seven years old, his lungs shot, his feet so swollen he could barely walk, he never missed a beat, much less a session. My workshops are intensely physical, and yet this frail giant explored all the phases of the movements and immersed himself in the massage and ritual theater work. He was able to play with his prodigious intellect and vast knowledge and simply *be* in what he was doing. His mind was both full and empty.

I well remember the first lecture I gave which he attended. I was totally intimidated by his presence; I knew that he had one of the most profound minds of our time. Yet he sat down right in front of me like an enthusiastic grade-school boy, and so charmed me with his attentiveness and boundless curiosity that I found myself opening up new facets of my thinking. His genius was contagious. His presence and acknowledgment have been an inspiration to me ever since.

The last time I saw him, as he lay dying in the hospital, his first words were, "Gabrielle, I won't be dancing with you again." He said it with grace, dignity, and only a hint of wistfulness.

Gregory and I—the thinker and the dancer, a most unlikely duo—met on a common ground, coming from different directions. We had both spent our lives investigating what Gregory called "the patterns which connect." I call them maps, maps to choreograph our energy and lead us to ecstasy, wholeness. Gregory's work was intellectual, mine physical. I'm sure he understood mine better than I his. But his validation of my intuitive discoveries was a crucial inspiration, and it was he who first urged me to write this book.

Ritual theater work soon became my focus. I started an experimental theater company to dig through the ruins of our contemporary psyches, to probe for truth, to find a level of authenticity that seemed to be missing. The people who gathered to do this work became an ensemble of true warriors as we ritualized and dramatized our journey through the inner terrain of the psyche. The work became an ongoing daily process that lasted three years and constantly reflected the ever-changing life experience and concerns of the performers.

I called this work-in-progress "Mirrors," as I called the company itself. "Mirrors" was the story of a doctor, a lawyer, a nobody, a hairdresser, a go-go dancer, a fairytale princess, a free-lance-metaphysical-existentialist, and a shaman, all trapped in a one-act play in which the performers and audience could witness themselves with humor and compassion. We performed it for audiences of thousands and for audiences of only a few dozen. We performed it in theaters, lofts, churches, and union halls. We performed it in the cities and in the country, in the West and in the East. Wherever we were, the setting was the human ego. The time was now. The place was everywhere. It was cathartic work, and it became a rite of passage for each of us.

And, my work deepened as I began to understand it, to see the relationships among its elements. The theater experiment was a lab—a place to research my obsession with what it really means to be a human being, a whole one. We turned our lives into art, into dances, into songs, into poems, into theater—and this was the healing.

"Mirrors" also became a band, an urban primitive rock 'n' roll band devoted to making trance music. I began to map the journey from inertia to ecstasy in rhythm and music at the same time as I was dramatizing it. Endless hours in the recording studio, under serious pressure, eating turkey on rye at 3:00 A.M., looking for the ways to ecstasy through modern technology.

Music is essential to the modern shamanic journey. It is the inspiration, the guide, the calling. It holds our stories, our myths, our hearts and souls. It speaks to the spirit of our times. Many of my favorite shamans are rock stars. They probably don't even know they're shamans but they know how to get to ecstasy and back, and how to take others with them. They may not have a license, but they know how to drive.

Many shamans have been born and have died in the beat of rock 'n' roll—charting their journeys, dancing their demons in concert stadiums all over the world. When we're lucky, they take us along with them.

Rock 'n' roll has become a universal form of music. It moves beyond boundaries, beyond politics, beyond religion, economics, culture, sociology, language, custom, and ideology. Rock 'n' roll speaks to the soul of freedom. It is today's shamanic call—back to the beat, the heartbeat, back to the body, back to basics.

Rock for the rain forests, for starving children and burned out farmers—rock for the homeless, rock for political prisoners. Rock it, roll it, change it.

Rock concerts are the modern tribal rituals where communal ecstasy is a real possibility—the moment when the crowd and music are one, in the beat. This is religious experience, holy communion. Our young people are starving for unity and this is their hope. How wonderful that it all takes place in a context where all we're being sold is T-shirts—not guilt, obligation, hierarchy, stricture, or dogma.

All rock stars aren't shamans. All shamans aren't rock stars. But it's a good place to be for a modern shaman and the ones out there now are speaking to the planet as a whole. Their songs cut to the universal core, touch us where we all live, inspire us. Rock 'n' roll shamans chart the journey with poetry and sound, but mostly with energy. They speak to us below the mind and have taken me on my journeys again and again—they've been the strongest allies in my work.

———

You really need to dance through this book. Dance in between the lines. It is, in itself, a shamanic journey, an initiation. It calls on you to discover and explore your own shamanic self. It doesn't require going out and buying feathers or even beating a drum. But it demands listening to the beat of your own heart; finding your own rhythm; singing your own blues; writing your own story; acting out your own fantasies; and seeing your own visions. This is a contemporary, urban-primitive, western-Zen, right-now trip. It's a journey into wholeness, an initiation into a shamanic perspective.

This book initiates you into the five sacred powers natural and necessary for survival—the power of being, the power of loving, the power of knowing, the power of seeing, the power of healing. These are the real powers. Most of us are actually afraid of real power. True aliveness is rare, and experiencing it is like being jolted out of a long sleep. But we have to overcome our fear, if we are to wake up from the living death of muted existence.

I offer you a shamanic practice for body, heart, mind, soul, and spirit. It's not offered as gospel. It's just a door to open, through which you may see yourself, an opportunity to free your body, express your heart, empty your mind, awaken your soul, and embody your spirit.

Have a great trip.

ONE

Freeing the Body

THE POWER OF BEING

---

ain't it strange

hand of god feel the finger/hand of god I start to whirl
hand of god I don't linger/don't get dizzy/do not fall now
turn whirl like a dervish/turn god make a move/turn lord
I don't get nervous oh I just move in another dimension

come move in another dimension
come move in another dimension

Patti Smith[3]

The first shamanic task is to free the body to experience
the power of being.

It is first in that it is both where we must begin and
what is most fundamental. Your body is the ground metaphor of your life, the expression of your existence. It is your
Bible, your encyclopedia, your life story. Everything that
happens to you is stored and reflected in your body. Your
body knows; your body tells. The relationship of your self
to your body is indivisible, inescapable, unavoidable. In the
marriage of flesh and spirit, divorce is impossible, but that

doesn't mean that the marriage is necessarily happy or successful.

So the body is where the dancing path to wholeness must begin. Only when you truly inhabit your body can you begin the healing journey. So many of us are not in our bodies, really at home and vibrantly present there. Nor are we in touch with the basic rhythms that constitute our bodily life. We live outside ourselves—in our heads, our memories, our longings—absentee landlords of our own estate. A brochure I saw at a chiropractor's office says: "If you wear out your body, where are you going to live?"

One incident in my search always sticks out for me: I ran into a rabbi in a shopping mall. We got to talking and I asked, "Do Jews hate their bodies as much as Catholics?" He started to laugh in mock shock, but then gave me a more quizzical look. It seemed I'd hit on something close to him. He told me that he'd just buried his father, who was also a rabbi. He'd asked his father on his deathbed, "What was the most important thing in your life, the Torah?" And the old man had answered, "My body." "I was stunned," his son now told me. He stared past me in awkward silence and finally said, "I always thought my body was just a vehicle for my mind; feed it, clothe it, send it to Harvard."

Being—existence, energy, vitality—means that our spirit fills our body. Our full self is embodied. But when we look in the mirror, what do we see? A dull, vacant stare? A sunken chest? A phony smile? Go take a look. What do you see? If it isn't a vibrant self brimming with energy and presence, then you're shortchanging yourself on the gift of life. I know. I've been there. I've seen thousands of absentee selves, and you have too—on the subway, in rush-hour traffic, in the supermarket, profiled in the eerie evening glow of the tube—and you know, all too often, you're one of them.

For many of us, the body is a feared enemy whose instincts, impulses, hungers are to be conquered, tamed, trained for service, beaten into submission.

Ironically, that's what I did as a "dancer"—I learned to ignore, deny, control, misuse, and abuse my body. I could make it do fancy steps, rev it up with one drug and knock it out with another, starve it and adorn it, but I didn't trust my body, I didn't like it. No wonder I didn't live in my body, or seldom let my breath move below my neck. Mine became a body disconnected from the waves, the rhythms, the cycles that comprised the ocean of my being. I could dance, but I'd forgotten how to really move or be moved.

My way back into life was ecstatic dance. I reentered my body by learning to move my self, to dance my own dance from the inside out, not the outside in. And over the years, I discovered—in observing my own body and thousands of others—the five sacred rhythms that are the essence of the body in motion, the body alive: *Flowing ..... Staccato ..... Chaos ..... Lyric ..... Stillness.*

1. THE FIVE SACRED RHYTHMS

The rhythm is below me
The rhythm of the heat
The rhythm is around me
The rhythm has control
The rhythm is inside me
The rhythm has my soul.

Peter Gabriel[4]

Picture a lone dancer—yourself—on a bare dark stage against a white backdrop. Standing perfectly still, quiet as night. You feel your breath rising and sinking, expanding and contracting. You let your head drop forward, feel its weight, let it roll around your shoulders, move up and down, from side to side. Heavy, slow movements that slide into your shoulders. Then your elbows. Slow, heavy movements carving shapes in space. Then your hands take over and do their own dance. Your hips catch the spreading fever, rock and roll, twist and turn around and around. Your knees bend and lift, describing small and large arcs. And finally your feet slide, stamp, tap—experimenting with a dozen ways of walking. All the parts of your instrument are tuned. Your body is primed for the five sacred rhythms.

The lights come up like dawn. Your body is still again. You feel the rise and fall of your breath, the expansion and contraction of your rib cage. You go with this *flowing* rhythm, enhance it, exaggerate: inhaling, rising, expanding, opening; then exhaling, sinking, contracting, closing. You ride this wave of movement again and again until you're stretching like a waking cat. Slowly the music of a lonely sax catches you in its sweet parabolas of sound, and you become a continuum of movement, creating an infinity of shapes as you move up and down, rising and sinking like a heavy sun. Breathing deeply in and out, there are no sharp edges to your movements, only curves, endless circles of motion, each gesture evolving into the next. Your body has become a sea of waves—powerful, constant rhythmic motion rooted in the earth, relaxed and centered, *flowing* in all directions.

Then the drums come in, and the other horns, bursting the half-waking dream with pulsating energy. It's as if you're caught in a sudden storm, waves pounding, your body being carried by the tempo. You begin to move in sharp, *staccato*, defined ways, each movement having a beginning and end. You fuse with the beat of the drums, and your arms and legs become percussive instruments, beating the floor and the space around. You're *staccato* incarnate, torso twisting sharply, arms flashing, feet pounding, one with your pulse, living on air, exhaling into one movement, and breathing life in with the next. Your body's jerking, jabbing, jamming, falling into patterns and repeating them over and over till they die and some new pattern is born—like the music of Philip Glass. You're doing body jazz.

Now the beat builds, the pace quickens. You're going over the edge into *chaos*. You lose control. Get drowned by the beat. The lights are flashing, the stage spinning. You're swept up in some primal rite, falling deeper and deeper into yourself, a waking trance. The Kodo Heart Beat Drummers are blasting through the speakers. Your body's gyrating, limp as a drunk ragdoll, spine undulating, head loose, hands flying, feet locked in the beat. You're electric, turned on, plugged into some huge transformer. You're flashdancing your heart out, brain in neutral, vibrantly alive, and totally *chaotic*.

But just when you think you're going to burst, or collapse, you land like a feather on the light side of yourself in *lyrical* rhythm. The lights melt into a pastel glow, violins swell into a sweet tune, and your body sweeps into graceful loops as winning as a waltz. This *lyric* mood is delicious as fresh fruit, lulling as a summer breeze, playful as an otter. Breezy, light on your feet, you swirl Isadora-like more and more slowly till stillness comes.

You drop to the floor, feel your breath rising and falling, expanding and contracting. *Stillness* is full of being. Being alive. You feel radiant, transformed, ecstatic. Your body's *still*, but inside everything's alive with movement.

Catch the rhythms? Recognize them? I'm sure you do. Just think of the best lovemaking you ever experienced. Strong and *flowing*, gentle and slow, lingering and tender in its foreplay; pulsing and full of energy, pounding *staccato* passion and captivating tension as the sexual fever builds; wild, *chaotic*, out of control, beyond all thinking and fears with the onset of orgasm; sweet basking in the loving, *lyrical* security of perfect arms and the luscious afterglow of the best it ever gets; and finally, *stillness*, tranquil as dusk light when everything becomes clear and gorgeous in the silhouetting of sunset.

Or recognize the rhythms in the birth of a child. Labor begins with gentle, undulating movement in the womb; builds into strong, stabbing contractions; crescendos with impossible, body-engulfing pains and the final bursts of pressure that whoosh the baby out and send joy racing through every cell, culminating in the ecstatic stillness of embracing your nursing infant.

Over the years I've found that these rhythms—flowing, staccato, chaos, lyric, stillness—constitute the fluid structure, the DNA, of our physical lives. We know from physics that everything is in motion, and that the authentic way of understanding reality is to think in terms of motion: rhythms, vibrations, frequencies—the language of constant change, of flux.

So our challenge is to become conscious of these rhythms, to truly experience them, to enter into them. We have to learn to know what rhythm we're in, how to ride with it, how to shift; to sense what rhythm others are in and how the different rhythms are complementary or discordant. We need to discover what rhythm predominates in us—are we a flowing type, a chaotic type? What rhythms characterize the main people in our lives? We need to tune into the undulating rhythms of our days, our weeks, our months, our years.

2. Doing the Rhythms

So how do we get in touch with the rhythms that are our body's native language? The simplest answer is to "do the rhythms," to act them out, enter into them. And the simplest, most natural way to do them is to dance them. There are no rules or fixed instructions, because ultimately your own body, your own energy, is your teacher.

Dance is the most immediate way of expressing the body's essential rhythms; dance is spontaneous, universal—watch how children respond to music, and remember that every human culture has its dance forms, embodying the varying rhythms. In my workshops, I provide appropriate music for each rhythm and invite participants to discover their own expression of them: the flowing, contour-following rhythm that may look like tai chi or moving through honey—slow, mellifluous, elegant; the sharp, defined, syncopated karate-like moves of staccato; the wild tribal, out-of-your-head, carnival blowout that is chaos; the light, airy, dancing-on-air of the lyric phase; and the mime-like dialectic between movement and stasis that is dynamic stillness. The spontaneous choreography by people who have never been formally trained in dance constantly astonishes me: it's as fresh, bold, and inventive as most work I've seen done by dance troupes.

Anyone can do the rhythms. They are in us, and are part of our essential makeup; they just need to be evoked, to find expression in our own unique beings. I've worked with everybody—rock stars and priests, kids and old people, schizophrenics and uptight intellectuals—and they all discover the dancer within as the procession through the rhythms liberates their limbs and they rediscover their body. I've "taught" thousands, and there's never been one who couldn't master the rhythms.

Even my friend Stanley. In 1975, I did a lecture/demonstration at the big Unitarian church in San Francisco. Afterward a sixty-five-year-old man, who had been in an industrial explosion that had left him half deaf and severely palsied, came up to me very excitedly and told me in slurred speech how thrilled he was about the dance. So I invited him to come to the next workshop I was giving. He came, and he's been working with me ever since. In the course of the last twelve years, by regularly doing the rhythms, he's been able to move beyond his palsied, spastic condition and to open and expand his movements and his speech.

Stanley has been like a withered flower coming back into bloom. When I first met him, his arms were contracted tight against his chest, his hands were tight-fisted like gnarled clubs, and his body was shaking in a perpetual state of chaos. In doing the rhythms, Stanley entered into this chaotic state and from there, found his way into the other rhythms—first staccato, then flowing, then lyrical, and finally achieving a kind of stillness—gradually reintroducing his body to its other ways of being. Doing the rhythms relaxed him tremendously and opened him up to the whole repertoire of human movement. His progress, needless to say, has made all the difference in the quality of his life and has been a joyful discovery for me. Stanley has become a grandfather spirit of my work. He now wears dance clothes and funny little hats, and he's not only picked up the spirit of dance but developed his own distinctive style. Going strong at eighty, he's discovered the dance of life and is a constant joy and inspiration.

People are surprised to discover that the rhythms are not only healing but also energizing and relaxing. In exploring the full range of our body's natural movement, we reconnect with our native animal energy, and start to be present in our bodies.

In my workshops I use live or taped music appropriate to each rhythm and briefly demonstrate how each rhythm looks and feels, how it can be embodied. Sometimes I don't use music at all and instead encourage people to follow their own inner sense of rhythm. I don't teach steps—your body has its own steps, its moves, its own ways of being in each rhythm; you discover your dance by doing it. I have put together a tape of my own music to accompany this book ("Initiation") and to lead you through the five rhythms. But you can make your own rhythm tapes. It's important for you to discover what moves *you*.

It's ideal to set aside the same time every day, five days a week, and devote that time to doing the rhythms. Find a time structure that works for you—morning, afternoon, or evening. The ritual of your movement work is up to you. If you don't want to do the rhythms every day, do them when the spirit moves you. You can do the rhythms alone or with others. For some it's a daily meditation. For others, it's exercise. For me, it's both.

You'll want to wear light, loose-fitting clothing and light shoes you can dance in, or just bare feet. You can put on my rhythms tape, starting at the beginning of side one. Or put on some smooth, undulating music of any kind. It's the *flowing* rhythm that's important, not whether it's rock or classical or ethnic. Tune into the music, let it penetrate you. Feel its pulse, its contours, its waves. Music is an ally, an inspiration, a lure: it spontaneously evokes our inner rhythms and induces our body into movement. Gradually begin moving with the flowing rhythm of the music. Stretching, undulating, feeling the weight of each movement in space, you're inventing your own tai chi. You feel your feet firmly on the floor and the circular movements of your legs, your arms, and your hands describe an evolving continuum. You're centered in your belly and all the movement begins and returns there: rising on the inhale, exaggerated and prolonged, and sinking and contracting on the exhale through the mouth. Just flow with the music as the spirit moves. There's no right way to do it, only your way. And gradually your own style, your unique way of being, will emerge, and the movements, and the breathing, and the flow of the music will blend into a dynamic unity so that you will feel you are the rhythm, you are flowing.

Next you move into *staccato* following my tape or whatever music you choose that has a hard, driving, pulsating beat. Let the beat take hold of you. Then, inhaling with each movement and letting out the breath explosively, making whatever sounds come out, your movements become fast-paced, thrusting, pounding—each movement isolated, with a beginning and an end. You're moving in lines and angles, no longer in circles, and your moves are percussive, short; they've got edges, and your breath releases in bursts of sound. As in every other rhythm, if you put your mind and your concentration in your feet, the waves will flow through your whole body and you'll become more and more aware of all the parts of your body as they're swept into the beat.

To move into *chaos*, I love to be carried away by tribal African drumming. Chaos is rooted in flowing and staccato rhythms but revs them up beyond control. Jerks, spins, releases, taking every movement over the edge, yet totally grounded in your feet. You're carried away, surrendering to the surging and darting of the music. Letting the brain and the controlling mind go, and letting the body loose—no blocks, no inhibitions, no doubts, just pure animal gyrations. All by yourself, who's to care? Go for it!

And the storms of chaos lead ineluctably to the rainbow glow of the *lyrical* phase. The mood of the music is light, bouncy, exhilarating. The moves are airy, playful; your feet hardly touch the floor, all effortless gliding, swinging, twirling. You're as light-footed as a deer; everything is exploratory, delighting. It's the moving of serene joy, of celebration.

Finally comes *stillness*. But not inertia or sedentary intransigence. The movement becomes inner, a feeling of empty fullness, of concentration, of vibrant presence. You move in slow motion, or you move and stop, move and stop, feeling your feet, your face, your hands, your total body. No longer is the movement the meditation, but the stillness between. It can look like mime or like breakdancing. Move and stop. Hold. Move and stop. The breath is strong, the vitality intense. The time is now, the place here. Every gesture total, measured, your body full of breath, your look direct.

People practicing the rhythms regularly experience dramatic improvements in well-being. One student of mine used to hold all the stress and tension in her life in her lower back. When things got really tough in her life as a high-powered business school professor and corporate consultant, her back would go into spasms. Robin would have to lie in bed for days until her spasms relaxed. As this condition kept recurring and eventually led to her being hospitalized and put in traction several times, the doctors wanted to operate. But after doing the rhythms for several months, her whole body started to loosen up. Now, whenever her back starts seizing up, she moves gently through the rhythms rather than giving in to the spasms, and the tension eventually subsides. She starts with flowing movements and gradually moves into and through the stress. She has never returned to the hospital for traction, and of course has never had to have an operation. This fiercely ambitious woman had to be literally knocked off her feet and virtually paralyzed with pain before discovering that movement is the healer.

In doing the rhythms, many people tend to find one or more very natural and easy and another daunting and difficult. People in our culture tend to take readily to flowing and staccato, but balk at entering chaos, and find lyrical foreign to them. It's vital to enter into the rhythms we naturally resist, because they represent the lost dimensions of our being. Robin, for instance, was so resistant to experiencing chaos that she would get nauseated whenever we began the chaotic phase. I would find her hunched over in a corner holding her stomach. She was terrified of losing control, of surrendering—on the dance floor, in bed, or in her life generally. But such surrender is essential to our emotional and sexual lives, and to experiencing things deeply in whatever sphere. So pay attention to your resistances and dare to explore these undiscovered regions of yourself. One way is to start just with the music, perhaps with earphones, and let it get deep inside you; gradually you'll discover your innate capacity for this rhythm and this discovery will benefit you enormously.

We all tend to feel most at home in one particular rhythm or some combination of rhythms. For instance, I spontaneously operate in a flowing rhythm. It's good to find out what rhythm predominates in you in order to understand how you can best relate to other people, to places, to situations. If you're a flowing type and your husband, say, is a staccato personality, as mine is, realizing this difference in basic rhythm allows you to understand how you constantly interrelate—one person is always dashing off, totally goal-oriented, while the other saunters along taking everything in. In realizing the differences, you can learn how to create the best music of your life together.

Understanding the rhythms will open you up to new perceptions. You will become attuned to the rhythm of places and understand that New York is a staccato city, while Jamaica is lyrical. You can figure out how to link your energy with the pulse that's going on around you at the moment. Being unconsciously staccato in a still place means being totally out of sync. And this unconscious mismatching of rhythms goes on all the time, with lovers who constantly get on each other's nerves, unaware that one is operating in one rhythm and the other in another, or with people who live in places that slowly drive them crazy. You need to catch the rhythms of people, places, times of the year, the week, the day, and learn to dance with them.

So what rhythm are you? The easiest way to find out is to do the rhythms and discover which feel most natural, most your own. You may discover you've been living one way—say, very driven, staccato or in constant emotional chaos—but your real natural rhythm is another one. It's also easy to recognize dominant rhythms in others—your family, your friends, celebrities. Each person's essential rhythm is like his or her signature or fingerprint. The way people move is the way they are. Since we are complex beings, we can blend into heady mixes of the rhythms, such as flowing/chaos, staccato/lyrical, or any other combination.

I consider doing the rhythms a shamanic practice, but dance is not the only way. Once you begin to explore the rhythms through regular practice, you can easily find many other ways to do them. For example, you can *run* the different rhythms—from flowing strides through pounding running, to light stepping and the deliberate pacing of cooldown. Or you can do aerobics in each rhythm or swim, skate, or even sing them. One person who has worked with me privately sings the rhythms as he drives along, safe in the privacy of his car to hum, chant, belt out lyrics. This man is a Wall Street lawyer who suffers from a generalized ennui that leaves him stuck in intense inertia, his face impassive, his voice lifeless, his outlook bleak. But as he does the rhythms—dancing them, singing them—movement comes back into his face, light comes into his eyes, energy into his step, serenity and enthusiasm into his voice. This no-nonsense man, who hates all psychobabble and New Age talk, tells me that doing the rhythms is like being taken over by a force from within that is fresh and invigorating but somehow natural and his own, like making love without sex, like feeling a sense of your soul. He speaks about this experience with a kind of ecstatic glow he can't believe he's experiencing. The rhythms do lead to the ecstasy of reconnecting with the spirit of your body, and the ways of exercising them are many and varied. All that's needed is the willingness to do them.

3. RHYTHM MASSAGE

Another way of putting the rhythms into practice, of incorporating them into the body, is that of rhythmic massage: it allows the rhythms of flowing and stillness to be deeply experienced in the body and is an extremely beneficial and satisfying way of becoming rhythmically attuned to another person. Massage is a wonderful opportunity for us to keep in touch—literally—with our self, our mates, lovers, friends, and children, to heal with our hands. Massage is not a luxury for the rich or an indulgence of mellow sensualists or a euphemism for paid sex; it's a vital rhythmic interplay that should be a part of everybody's life.

Rhythmic massage releases the body—of both the giver and the recipient—into its essential energy flow. It reconnects us to our natural energy channels and unblocks what has been dammed up, both physically and psychologically. It engenders wholeness, ecstatic relaxation, and brings our consciousness out of our heads and into our whole body.

This massage involves atmosphere, attitude, and awareness. It can be practiced by anyone and requires no special training or techniques, just the willingness to give and to care for another (and correlatively, the willingness on the part of the recipient to receive and be nurtured).

First, create a peaceful *atmosphere*. Make sure that you won't be disturbed. Make the room warm and pleasing; you can use candles, soft light, soothing music, incense, flowers. Experiment to discover how to create a Shangri-la in space and time, an ideally pacific vacation in the midst of everyday living. The massage can be done on a massage table, a bed, or even the floor. You'll need massage oil—a light oil, like almond or sesame, is good and readily available at health food stores, body shops, etc.—and some thick towels.

Second, realize that *attitude* is the most important ingredient. You need to come with an attitude of love and service, wanting to give the other person an experience that he or she can never have alone. The energy of giving and receiving is circular. The surrendering to giving and the surrendering to receiving feed each other to build up a strong circuit of healing energy. Really giving yourself to massaging means feeding the other person with your energy, your spirit.

Soon after I started to give massages at Esalen, I came to realize that massage wasn't simply a physical, sensory process but a religious experience. It involved loving my neighbor as myself in the most concrete way, giving these people an integrated experience of their own bodies. I eventually ran the massage team at Esalen, and increasingly saw our work as a kind of daily monastic prayer. I was always meeting new bodies, often never saying a word to them but having this deep encounter with each. It was wonderful training in "impersonal" love, love without attachment, strings, complications—just deep giving and receiving in a circle of sharing. In doing it I discovered a deep, divine part of myself, and a capacity for generosity and for connecting that I'd never glimpsed before. And the rhythmic body prayer of massaging proved as healing and integrating to me as the people being made whole under my touch.

The third critical factor in giving a massage is *awareness*. Be aware of how relaxed you are. You shouldn't massage someone if you are in a state of nervous tension since you will end up instilling your negativity in the other person. It's important to be loose, natural, relaxed. One way of achieving that state is to do the rhythms briefly beforehand in order to come to the massage in a condition of energized calm. As the massage proceeds, remain aware of your own state of being, remembering yourself as you go along so that the process unfolds like an act of physical meditation.

You need to be fully aware of the other person as well. Before even putting your hands on the body, stand back and take it in: notice the body's shape, tuning into what it says about the person. Watch the body move, the breath rise and fall. Attend to every detail. You can see whether the shoulders are held tightly together, or whether the buttocks are hunched up, holding tension, or the legs, hands, and so on. You need to observe this unique body, paying attention to it as if it were the only body in the world besides your own, so that you do not end up applying some one-size-fits-all technique but will engage with this distinct body/person as he or she is here and now. The aim is to blend with it, to partner it like a dancer.

I speak of the body as "it" just as shorthand, but part of the awareness in any healing massage, of course, is that the body is an integrated body/spirit in which the physical, emotional, mental, and spiritual are all intertwined in a mysterious unity that transcends understanding, but can be experienced.

Begin with the body on its belly. Make sure that it is warm, comfortable, covering with towels the parts not being touched. Put a rolled-up towel under each ankle to take the pressure off the knees. You can check to make sure the person is completely comfortable and relaxed and use additional towels where necessary. Once the person is comfortable, just stand or sit at the feet of the body. After tuning into it carefully, hold the feet with both your hands, and just breathe, being there with the person. Gradually your breath will synchronize with the other's, and you can relax every part of your body in turn.

Notice that the body can be divided into parts: feet, legs, buttocks, back, arms, hands, shoulders, chest, stomach, pelvis, neck, and head. You can subdivide these sections into the calf, the knee, the thigh; the two halves of the back divided by the spine; the parts of the arms, the hands, the head, the chest, etc. It's not up to you to change or shift the body in any way; rather the need is to honor what is, to see the shape of the consciousness expressed in this body, and to affirm it: to say "yes" to this body, to this foot, to this leg, and so on. And your mental attitude should run along these lines: "This is your hand and it is beautiful. It is perfect in its own way just as a tree or a leaf or a snowflake or a kitten is beautiful and perfect if seen just for its own sake." This is the essential message the massage is giving: each part of the person is perfect, special, to be nurtured, cherished. Feel each part, appreciate each, breathe into each through your hands, love every dimension of the body before you. Just attending to the body in this way will settle the breathing into an easy pattern and heighten your awareness.

The essential ingredient in the touching, stroking, pulling, and kneading of massage is to be complete. You need to move from joint to joint in careful sequence—from ankle to knee, from knee to upper thigh, etc. Otherwise the person being massaged always experiences what is left untouched, missed, skipped over. If you're doing the foot, do the whole foot. Follow the contours, the crevices, and promontories of every part of the body, exploring them deeply, thoroughly. Breathing in harmony with the person, you need to truly give yourself, put yourself into the massaging, giving your own weight and pressure to each stroke. The worst thing you can do is slide haphazardly over the top of the skin without really penetrating, without delivering the whole of your self into the process. Random surface touching feels terrible. You will also want to use just enough oil so that the hands can move deeply and smoothly over the body.

With a moderate amount of oil warming on your hands and with a firm resolve to do everything completely, with real pressure and attention, you enter into the flowing rhythm of simple, circular repetition, a mantra of movement. Start with the left foot, holding it under your right hand. Follow its every contour with your massaging left hand, creating smooth circular rhythms, while holding it loosely in an appreciatively caressing grasp. Move with flowing grace, using not only your hand but the full sweep of your forearm. Kneading, pulling, stroking, applying enough pressure to deeply penetrate but not so much as to dig in or to disrupt the flow.

Then you can apply long flowing strokes to the rest of the left leg up to the buttocks, gradually adding more sections—first the foot and lower leg, then from the toe to the thigh—integrating more and more of the body into the rhythmic flow. Moving up and down, giving your weight and pulling in toward your own center, your own belly. Then, after you've done this several times, you can start to go over the buttock and include that portion in the elongated flowing strokes down through the whole leg. Repetition is the key. Once you're satisfied that you've energized and integrated the left leg, you stop and hold the left foot once again and affirmingly sense its vitality. Next you follow with the right leg, doing the same thing in a concentrated, unhurried dance of your hands, embracing the leg from the tip of the toe to the top of the thigh in expanding increments. Then you go from the tip of each foot using both hands to embrace both legs, thighs, and buttocks in sweeping, integrating strokes. Remember to apply more oil as needed so that your strokes are smooth, but not slippery. Then you stop again, holding both feet, and you breathe and rest, and "be there."

When fully relaxed and synchronized again, you move up to the left side of the back, applying long flowing strokes again and again, up to the shoulder and down the left side of the body. Once that side is awakened under your touch, you then hold the left hand between yours and stop and breathe for anywhere from one to three minutes. Then move to the right side of the back and do the same thing from the top of the buttock up to the shoulder. After holding the right hand as you did the left, put your hands at the base of the spine, with your two thumbs on either side of the spine, and go up the long muscle of the back pressing in firmly, continuing over the shoulders and down the arms to the hands, doing this over and over again. Then, position yourself at the head and do the same thing. Once you've awakened the back side of the body, you can go back to the feet, go all the way up the left side of the body, and then the right, from the tip of the feet to the tip of the fingers. Then you can move to working on the neck, feeling the grooves and the channels of energy to get them flowing, relieving the knots of tension, rubbing and relaxing the neck muscles.

Now turn the person over and begin the front side of the massage. Again start at the feet, holding them in the same way as before and gradually proceeding to work on the feet, legs, thighs, first one, then the other, then both together. Next you go to the head and place your hands right below the throat going down the chest and coming back up each side, then down the arms and in on the hands, in the course of which you massage the full chest, including the breasts, all the way down to the pubic bone in long, rhythmic, pushing and pulling strokes. Then you could lift both arms so that they're hanging behind the body, and work on each side of the body where the hips and thighs come together, then all the way up each side and down the arms to the tips of the hands. This is done while breathing very deeply and having the person take a deep breath, a big inhale and slow exhale. You can finish by working on the head and the various parts of the face, where we often hold a lot of tension.

When you're finished, you can sit on one side and put your hand approximately three fingers below the belly button and just be there with your hand firmly on the stomach for five to ten minutes while breathing easily. You'll feel the stomach coming up and literally pushing your hand off the body, which indicates that you have drawn the breath deep into the belly. This connecting is a deep mothering, a nurturing experience for both giver and receiver. It can be used in many situations—to calm a child or a friend in distress, to express a special connection with the love of your life. It is a deep healing gesture that calls the spirit into the body, the breath into a naturally full rhythm. You can even do this for yourself: lie on your back, feet planted firmly on the floor, knees up, hands on belly, and breathe through your body into your hands.

Massage is a delicious way of making contact. It is designed to bring the body into a deep state of relaxation that is the vibrant obverse of sleep—flowing movement eliciting a state of vital peace. As you become more experienced in giving this kind of massage, you will develop techniques of your own and adapt your approach to each particular person. You can also incorporate other rhythms, such as the staccato kneading and chopping techniques of some kinds of massage—especially shiatsu, and the feathery lyrical touching that can be the perfect light finish to a deep massage.

This dynamic touching is something to do with your babies, your children, your lover, your friends, your parents. Sometimes you might just do a foot or a hand or a face. It is a great way to be in touch with those who matter most to us. We tend to be a lonely society, out of touch with even those who seem closest to us. This is the way to "reach out and touch someone"—a practical, healing path of generous and rewarding intimacy.

In addition to the closing technique of placing a hand on the belly, many of the others can and should be practiced on yourself. In fact, self-massage is a wonderful way to learn the art of rhythmic massage. Create the same atmosphere, adopt the same attitude of love and service, carry through with the same deep awareness. Begin with your foot and work your way up your leg, then your other foot and leg, following your own contours, your own shape with the loving caresses of your own hands. You won't be able to include every area of your body—maybe that's why we pair off into couples—but you can massage most of yourself. You can learn from working on yourself just how much pressure feels good, the joys of repetition and completion, how wonderful it feels to be touched, loved, cared for. Often we need to treasure ourselves as much as anyone else; so much suffering is ultimately rooted in people not caring for themselves.

Profound massage does bring up a lot of sexual energy, especially if such energy is repressed or only superficially expressed. So it is best to keep a towel over the genital area during the massage so that the massage provides a full rhythmic exchange rather than moving inappropriately or prematurely into the highly charged realm of sexuality. If sexual feelings do come up, as is often the case, the person can be advised not to fight them but simply to feel them as waves of vital energy that pass. It is most valuable to explore massage as a nonsexual way of body-to-body sharing and intimacy, getting to a deeper and deeper level of bodily consciousness than we can get to by ourselves. In following the bodily shape of the consciousness with loving and flowing strokes, we communicate a message we all need to hear, to feel again and again: "You are enough. You are perfect in your own way."

4. THE RHYTHMS OF LOVEMAKING

Another key way of freeing the body to experience the true power of being is the full expression of the sexual energy that courses through us, that drives us forward. One of the most vital tasks in our lives, in order to come fully into our human power, is to *learn how to make love.* It is something we are never taught in our puritanical/prurient culture, at least not until well into our twenties, and then, accidentally and rarely. There are still too many people—most, in fact—walking around out there who cannot make love in any sort of complete and satisfying way. Ours is a supposedly liberated, even libertine culture, but it is actually woefully underdeveloped sexually. It substitutes rampant titillation and hit-and-run sex acts for thorough sexual experience. It's well worth wondering what sort of world ours would be—how much less violence, rape, addiction, depression, crime, and war—if people were regularly having rich, full sexual experiences. We are surrounded by attempts to achieve sexual satisfaction in almost every way possible except the deeply rewarding one. How many of us know how to have a total, full-body, cathartic, shaking-all-over sexual experience?

Full sexual experience is the most fundamental way of healing ourselves. It releases all the tensions and stress that build up in us, and we end up embraced by and embracing the world in the person of our lover. But most of the sex all around us—in advertising, entertainment, furtive encounters in the dark—tends to be external and superficial, more in the head than in the body. This chronic abuse of sexuality is as noxious and destructive as true sexual experience is healing, whole-making. We talk and think a lot about sex, but mostly we don't do it well.

The most basic thing we need to do is to slow down the lovemaking process. It's not something that can be squeezed in between the news and Johnny Carson, the 7 A.M. alarm and the dash to work. Making love takes time. We must give it the time such a vital ingredient of our well-being deserves, which means that sex is probably not best engaged in every day. You want the energy to build so when you do it, you do it with full commitment and awareness, since this should be one of the sacred, inviolate dimensions of your life. There should be enough time and freedom to do nothing else but be lovingly sexual.

The key, of course, is the rhythms—expressing sexual energy through the full range of the five rhythms. In a sense, the most vital aspect of my work is evoking people's capacity for having total orgasms. Again and again, participants in my movement workshops tell me that it was only after they started doing the rhythms, experiencing the full dimensions of their bodies' energy patterns, that they were able to achieve total orgasm. And this discovery has recurrently led them to ecstasy and genuine life transformation. Doing the rhythms allows us to explore completely the phases of bodily energy—especially chaos, the loss of control we almost all dread—in a safe, congenial way and thus opens us up to the full dimensions of sexual experience, which is quintessentially rhythmical.

I jokingly call my approach to sex the "Roth Rhythm Method." The Catholic hierarchy has had the right term but the wrong idea—the rhythms are the language of lovemaking, not a kind of birth control. Full sexual being means experiencing the fullness of each rhythm in our sexual encounters. We are called to a gentle, pounding, wild, wonderful ride on the waves of sexual energy, tossing us up on the sands of paradise.

Try making love by starting with a leisurely interplay of flowing rhythms. The massage I just described is a great way to initiate the first act of the five-act play that true sex is. All that needs to be added is the erotic sensibility and sexual intentionality. Use music to catalyze the rhythm in your lovemaking. Rising and sinking with each other, sharing flowing, weighted caresses, exploring and affirming every part of each other's body in smooth, circular movements, and letting the energy slowly build as the body gets fully turned on and opened up. This is the way to sexual ecstasy.

Only when both bodies are fully opened in dynamic relaxation and energy is fully flowing, should the man enter the woman. Then the strong, slow, flowing movements continue inside and in our interlocking embraces. On their own, our bodies will move into a more staccato rhythm, the energy more percussive and insistent, the tension and excitement mounting. It is best just to let this pounding energy arise naturally without pushing, forcing, rushing. It will build and build, stronger and stronger, its juices sweeter and sweeter, until it bursts the dams of our control and overflows into a deep chaotic phase. Here we must surrender to the energy, let it take over; if we do, sounds and feelings will erupt unbidden, a passionate animal energy will possess us and take us where we've never been before. Best to give in to the thrill of the ride, the adventure, the ever-undiscovered country.

This surrender takes us to an even deeper level. It is there that the orgasm begins to build and there should be no rushing to finish, to cut short the sweet anxiety of waiting or the delicious plunge, that cellular explosion that comes at the peak. This explosion, if it is total, reverberates through our whole body, our whole being, releasing everything inside of us, freeing all our blocks.

With this total, body-shaking, eruptive, overwhelming orgasm we're swept onto a plateau of light, joyous intimacy. Post-coital tristesse, I'm convinced, is just a misguided romanticization of the dissatisfaction with "quickie" sex, an experience completely different from full, leisurely, expressive lovemaking. And with true orgasm, through surrender to chaos, there comes the lyrical phase: the genital connection remains, but the energy changes. We begin to caress and look appreciatively at each other again, honoring and cherishing anew.

Gradually let the energy calm into blissful, fulfilled stillness. Here lies the depth of our healing, this profound feeling of oneness, connection, exhilaration in being. Now comes the taste of ecstasy, of pure untrammeled joy, a space in time that is perfect and whole. How sweet it is, sexual ecstasy. And not the sort of experience that comes on a one-night stand: the whole movement to safe, responsible sex may have the unexpected benefit of making us learn how to truly make love to one another.

Clearly, doing the rhythms as movement and practicing the massage facilitate authentic lovemaking, the sexual experience we human beings are designed to have. Regular rhythmic practice plugs us into our body's dynamics—especially prolonged flowing and the surrender to chaos—that are vital to real "sexual healing."

It is also true that fully orgasmic sexuality requires an emotional freedom and an unfolding of our sexual development through its natural stages that are all too rare. If the heart is not free to experience the power of loving, if we are

emotionally blocked and holding back feelings, there is no
way we can experience total orgasm, or total well-being.
And if our sexual growth remains in a state of arrested
development, our full sexual capacities can only be tapped
by discovering where we got hung up and working rhythmically through each stage.

5. THE FIVE CYCLES OF SEXUAL DEVELOPMENT

Assuring realization of your sexual development requires healing reflection on your own sexual history. Our
sexuality matures through the five cycles of life (discussed
more fully in Chapter 3). We begin our sexual growth with
discovering our own body (in the birth cycle), expand sexual awareness (in the childhood cycle) through play with
friends, blossom (in the puberty cycle) into full sexual relationships with lovers, peak (in the maturity cycle) in
mating with a life lover, and internalize once again (in the
death cycle) with advancing age, wisdom, and experience.
You touch yourself, touch another, go all the way, bond with
someone, and finally let go. Each of the sexual cycles is
vital, each a preparation for the next. None can be missed
without leaving a deep hole in the psyche. So it is an essential task to take stock of your own sexual history so that
the sexual dimension of your life becomes a crucial aspect
of your work of freeing not only the body, but the heart,
mind, soul, and spirit as well.

In the initial five-year cycle of our lives, the body or
birth cycle, the thrust of our sexual energy is inward, as we
discover the wondrous, electrically charged body we are.
We learn to take food in and process it out, crawl, walk,
talk, play, all at the impetus of our primal life force, ground-
ing ourselves in our all-new physical world. We touch, pinch,

slap, poke, squeeze, and rub our bodies, sometimes aimlessly, sometimes intensely, as though a magnet pulls us toward ourselves. We play with our bodies, with our genitals, and the pleasure we experience in touching ourselves promotes the self-exploration vital to our sexual development. These moments with ourselves are the precious beginnings of all our sexual encounters. We learn to make contact with ourselves before we learn to touch others. First we make love to ourselves.

So many children are punished for playing with their own bodies, and this repression of natural instinct lies at the root of their subsequent sexual neuroses. If you were one of them, how could you learn to love and trust your own body if its impulses led to humiliation and punishment? How could you understand, with your innocent mind, how something so natural could be dirty and wrong? Being admonished for touching the body you live in makes no sense to an innocent mind.

How can such prohibition not establish a connection between sensual self-exploration and punishment? Won't it mean that you'll tend to spend your life repressing pleasure in order to avoid pain? Here's where the frigid and dull are born, so committed to not turning on that life itself appears to have drained from their bodies. Or will you tend to seek pain to find pleasure? Here is where pornography and perversion are born.

We are conditioned against acting out our love for ourselves; we believe we are unworthy. There we are in our little four- or five-year-old bodies, coerced into pitting ourselves against the very flow of nature, the primal force of life itself. Our bodies become our enemies, alien forces to be mistrusted and subdued. It becomes good to deny ourselves, bad to acknowledge our feelings. It becomes good to control; bad to surrender.

In the moment of punishment for self-exploration is the moment of our division: good/bad, mind/body, right/wrong.

Caught between what we feel and what we "should" do, we are cut off from our bodies, jolted out of the immediacy of our relationship to ourselves. We begin to think about it; sexuality becomes a matter of deliberation, weighing, doubts, fears, other people's agendas.

We can never really leave a cycle we do not complete. The sexual need's residual energy travels with us, and we become neurotically fixated on it. The impulse toward self-exploration and stimulation is real; we are destined to deal directly or indirectly with our natural needs until we incorporate them into our way of spontaneously being. Without an adequate foundation our adult life cannot be balanced sexually, and we find ourselves dominated by sex, by either its absence or excess. We may be in denial, our arms dead by our sides, pelvis tight, knees locked, fighting the devil of instinct in its many guises, or we may be sexually addicted, having sex without feeling or relationship, thinking about sex all the time, always looking for someone or something outside ourselves to turn us on when we are actually afraid for it to truly happen. Life becomes a living contradiction when we are conditioned to battle against its most fundamental energy from the first time it arose in us.

However, if we are allowed to love and explore ourselves in peace as infants and toddlers, with our sexuality being implicitly accepted and affirmed and integrated into our self-valuing and nurturing instincts, then we have a solid base from which to advance to the next sexual stage. The second stage of our lives, childhood, the heart cycle, from about ages five to ten, is the time for our sexuality to be expressed in exploration and play with friends of our own sex. This cycle begins when we align ourselves with our gender and consciously see ourselves as male or female. Generally, boys spend their time with boys and girls with girls. This pattern may be partially due to our conditioning, but it is also a natural impulse to begin to learn about what is outside of us through contact with others who are the most like us. Our first "love affair" is often with a best friend. It's usually a totally innocent relationship, although such friendships may on occasion verge into more explicitly sexual touching, and there are cultures where open sexual exploration between older children/teens of the same sex is readily accepted. Commonly, it amounts to wanting to be with the person all the time, sitting next to them, holding the friend's hand, spending nights over at each other's house. Our hearts open in the warm bond of friendship.

In childhood, sexual energy gets expressed mostly in tickling, hugging, leaning on, jumping on, grabbing one another, playing tag and hide-and-seek. There are the wide-eyed, surreptitious games of exploring others' bodies, playing "house" and "doctor." And the education in all this is more relational than physical: we're learning to relate as protosexual beings, extending our boundaries, experimenting with all kinds of contact with others, learning how to get along, hold our own, interact.

This phase of life processes sexual energy through the heart. When our friends are the medium for the initial outward expression of our sexual energy, when sexuality becomes swept up in personal interrelating, then we are blessed with the loving connection of sexuality and feeling, life energy and heart. Sexual energy that doesn't flow through the heart is always inappropriate; without heart, self-love yields guilt, friend-love becomes distorted, lovers become mere lust objects. When sex comes from the body, it is a necessity. When it comes from the mind, it is a fantasy. When it comes from the heart, it is love, our connection at the most sacred level. Sex is essentially meaningless without the heart.

Because of homophobia or residual puritanism, there is still a lot of uptightness about the special friendships and even the horseplay of childhood. But how can we ever really make love if we don't trust ourselves to make the most innocent, playful physical contact with our friends? We can't be true lovers if we don't learn first how to be friends, and we can't be friends if we are uptight about touching one another.

With the dawn of puberty our sexuality becomes powerfully self-conscious and of focal concern. It is then that we enter the cycle of adolescence, the period of becoming lovers. Nowadays it often lasts as long as twenty years. It is a time of experimentation and exploration; we are caught in powerful tides of self-creating energy that we need to channel in constructive ways. It is the time when we learn the art, science, and politics of making love. We come out. We come together. We come.

No matter what society's rules are, we experiment with expressing our burgeoning sexual energy, whether tentatively or boldly, fearfully or bravely, narrowly or broadly. We experiment with many ways of being in relationship, from first dates to one-night stands to living together. The focus is not on permanent relationships, on forever, but on now. Life is chaotic, unpredictable, exciting. And in this maelstrom we discover who we are as distinctive sexual beings.

In this age of AIDS and epidemic teen pregnancies, it is vital for teenagers not only to have safe-sex education, but to be given other outlets for the expression and development of their sensuality. It is tragic to cut our emotional growing years short by early teen pregnancies, teen marriages, and permanent jobs; we are not ready that early and we are sowing the seeds of lifelong frustration. The ideal is to afford teenagers myriad ways to explore and develop sensual expressiveness and flexibility and to encourage them to extend the foreplay of adolescence so that when intercourse actually happens, the experience will be deep and rich right from the start.

It's also important to reinforce what teenagers already know in their heart of hearts: that full sexual relationships should be in the context of genuinely loving friendship. In such relationships your lover becomes your sacred teacher. You and your partner mutually discover how to become lovers, how to have encounters that carry you through all the rhythms with full-body orgasms, the deep, exploding, releasing waves of vibrant energy transforming the inertia that breeds disease at all levels of your being.

Puberty denied will eventually have its day: better the appropriate time rather than disruptively later. Our culture is full of repressed teenagers who go through their puberty in their thirties or forties. Ignorance and fear turn adolescence into a time of restriction rather than experimentation, limitation rather than expansion. The upshot is impotence, frigidity, premature ejaculation, mechanical sex, and all the other sexual dysfunctions that hundreds of thousands seek relief from in later life. And if you don't spend your pubescent energy learning to be a real lover, you spend it in daredevil driving, belligerence, ambition, depression. You drink it, smoke it, narcotize it, stuff it, or starve it.

With any luck, we reach maturity ready for intimacy, ready to bond and make a family. If we've learned in the prior cycles what we needed to learn, the desire to mate is natural. Commitment is an unforced focusing, a once-and-for-all sharing, a total investment in a joint enterprise of body, mind, heart. And sex itself becomes less centered in staccato or chaotic rhythms, and becomes more a lyrical, tantric connection that plays the entire octave of our bodily potential and not just one or two repetitive notes.

But so many of us have been wounded along the way. And the only way to committed sexual intimacy, to the fullness of sexual ecstasy with the love of your life, is to complete the unfinished business of your earlier sexual stages: learning to love yourself without guilt; forging the vital link between friendship and sexuality by letting your friendships be sensual and your sexuality be truly giving and receiving; allowing yourself the exploration, the abandon, the searching that puberty demands. Otherwise, the sexual wounds, fears, doubts, ignorance, repression—of body, heart, or mind—undermine the best of committed relationships, even if they manage to last.

As we advance into old age and enter the last stage of our lives, our sexual energy again turns inward in vibrant celibacy. The celibacy of age does not mean we no longer make love, but that our lovemaking is much more than sexual, incorporating a thousand other forms of caring. And our erotic energy spreads through all our living. In our last waltz, all of life becomes our partner. This total eroticizing of life is the fullness toward which our sexual development naturally unfolds, but again it is possible only with the fulfillment of the earlier stages. But how wondrous it is when you can arrive at old age as the embodiment of complete sexual development and are free to be as totally in your body as you were as a young child, now enriched with awareness, friendship, self-mastery, and a spiritual connection to everything around you.

This chapter has focused on the body, the place where we begin and end, for all practical purposes. And, if you have a body, you are a dancer. The power to move your body in rhythm is yours to claim. The power to be sensuous, to have total orgasm, is yours to claim. The power to be in tune with the rhythm of life, its waves and cycles, is yours to claim. This is the power of your being, the presence and charisma we all want so much.

As you free your body to receive the power of being, all kinds of feelings start to flow—old feelings, new feelings, dark and light. Being alive is dangerous. It means feeling, feeling things you might not want to feel or thought you never would. Being alive means having a heart and expressing it. In freeing the body, we free the heart to experience the power of love—the task of the next chapter.

TWO

Expressing the Heart

THE POWER OF LOVING

If metal can be polished
to a mirror-like finish—
What polishing does the mirror
of the heart require?

Between the mirror and the heart
is this single difference:
The heart conceals secrets
while the mirror does not.

From *The Ruins of the Heart*
Jeláluddin Rumi[5]

The second major shamanic task is to express the heart, freeing the emotions to experience the power of loving.

Moving the body through the rhythms necessarily releases emotions. Freeing the body leads inevitably to freeing the heart. Emotions need to flow like the blood circulating in the body. When our emotional arteries are blocked, when our heart is jammed up, our whole life lacks élan, vitality. And trying to love without our emotions flowing is like trying to drive a car with a seized-up engine, or run a marathon with collapsed lungs. This chapter explores the nature of the emotions and the ways we can get them moving.

For people raised to express their feelings spontaneously and naturally, a dynamic emotional life is as natural as exercise is to athletes. But for those of us who learned early on to block, suppress, or deny many of our feelings, emotional expression initially can be as painful as it is for an out-of-shape athlete to get back into condition. In order to avoid getting hurt, we don't risk expressing our feelings. We habituate ourselves to a state of emotional inertia, a kind of pervasive numbness, a waking death that shields us from the pain, but also keeps us from the now-or-never joy of living.

In any case, trying to escape from our emotions is a vain exercise in self-deception. There is no way we can effectively deny our emotions, because they will manifest and express themselves in one way or another, no matter how much we resist.

Feelings are real. They are not ideas that can be turned off. They are not abstractions. They are physical manifestations of energy, uniting body and mind and bringing them to the moment. Unexpressed, repressed, or suppressed, this energy becomes toxic. Without release, it surfaces in lumps, clots, tumors, spasms, migraine headaches, and other symptoms of physical distress. It is now clear that the repression of feelings has medical consequences. A wide variety of recent research has shown that repressing emotions takes its toll on our health—"repressor" personalities are shown to be much more prone to disease. The only real option, the only healthy alternative, is to embrace our emotions, to befriend them, to make them our own, and to learn to experience and express them appropriately in the moment.

I work with five basic emotions: fear, anger, sadness, joy, and compassion. What most of us tend to do is avoid or deny the seemingly "negative" emotions of fear, anger, and sadness as a shortcut to the "positive" feelings of happiness and compassion. But there is no route to true joy and compassion except through the prior emotions, and all we get without the experience of fear, anger, and sadness are cheap imitations of joy and compassion—pleasantness and sentimentality.

We're all scared. We're all angry. We're all sad. That's a given. The question is, what are we going to do about it? Acknowledging and discovering our fear, anger, and sadness are a big step, because we usually deny them. We spend much of our precious life wandering around in a veil of lies, deceiving ourselves and others, living in lifeless unreality. It just doesn't work. Not really.

Many suppose that the path to enlightenment and self-mastery involves, if not denying, at least transcending our "negative" emotions. Shouldn't we rise above our baser instincts and ascend to the tranquil joy and compassion for all that is our natural right? I'm convinced that such transcending is simply a path to illusive equanimity that will be blown apart as soon as any real life challenge arises. If you think that you can transcend fear, anger, and sadness, try riding the A train from the top of Manhattan to the depths of Brooklyn at midnight and see how you do. Or go through the holocaust museum in Jerusalem, or spend a night on the streets of Calcutta.

Why would anyone want to transcend being real, being alive? Why would we not want to experience our heart? The basic emotions are vital to our survival and total well-being. The challenge is not to transcend them, but to transform our relationship to them. We need to befriend and express our feelings with purity and directness in the moment.

The false identification of enlightenment with transcendence of feelings is age-old. The story is told of the Tibetan master whose son had died. When the master's followers came to his house to offer their condolences, they found him in his garden crying. They were dumbfounded, assuming that if anyone could handle the death of a loved one with equanimity it would be their master. So they asked him, "Master, why are you crying?" Looking at them directly with eyes filled with tears, he said, "I am crying because my son has died and I am sad."

We are meant to feel. The problem is that we have been taught from our earliest days to edit and deny our emotions. Watch a two-year-old for a couple of hours. She'll cringe with fear at the appearance of a big bearded stranger; she'll blow up in anger and floor-pounding frustration when she's told she's got to wear a coat or is offered the wrong color crayon; she'll cloud over and erupt into buckets of tears when her father leaves her at day care; she'll whoop with delight when she plays catch; and she'll be the soul of comfort when her baby sister falls off the bed. Two-year-olds are powerhouses of emotions, testing their limits, discovering the range of their feelings, intoxicated with their own independent life-force. But all too soon the fit into social life is so tight that it knocks all the edges off, and we learn to deny, repress, equivocate, and mask our feelings. All this blocked emotional energy is stored up and finally bursts open out of all proportion to the situation, or gets rechanneled into self-destructive patterns of behavior.

The aim is to have the spontaneity and purity of a child's emotional responses without being driven by the windstorms of emotions as children are. What we want is what philosopher Paul Ricoeur calls "second naiveté": a freshness of response, a spontaneity that is seasoned with wisdom and experience. And to achieve this we have to let our emotions surface, get to know and appropriate them: have them flowing in our life so that we fear what really threatens us, get angry at what invades our integrity, cry when we get hurt, smile when it all goes right, and care about the real needs of others. When all this starts to happen, you begin to know something of what love is all about.

Love is emotional energy flowing rightly. It is the full range of emotions expressed appropriately, in the moment, honestly, directly. A lover is a child grown up.

When the poet Rilke was suffering severe bouts of depression, he was advised to seek psychiatric help. But he feared that if his demons were taken from him, so too would the angels of creativity disappear. In other words, he knew that to remain a poet he had to be willing to experience the full range of emotions. We're all artists, creating our lives and the worlds we live in, and the optimum choice is for the full palette of the emotional range. To befriend our feelings we can dance them, sing them, act them, write them, and paint them; we can creatively explore and celebrate them.

1. A MAP OF THE EMOTIONS

In my explorations over the years, in my own path of self-discovery and my work with thousands of students and clients, I've become familiar with the basic geography of the emotions. So I'll offer you my map to the territory, though everybody's emotional terrain is distinct and you'll have to discover your own peaks and valleys, rivers and dams, tributaries and dump sites. Still, I think the basic elements of our emotional worlds are much the same.

Feelings happen with or without our consent. We may pretend not to feel them, but we pay the consequences of our self-delusion by becoming a warehouse of useless, outdated emotions. We are stuffed with unresolved issues from the past, crowded with things that are wholly inappropriate to who we are now and what we're now doing. For such cluttered hearts, expressing the right emotion in just the right way is like trying to find just the book you're looking for in one of those down-at-the-heels used bookstores that is randomly jammed with publications since the last century—next to impossible. We need to clean out our emotional closets, pare down to vital emotional trim.

Feelings are neither positive nor negative; they simply are elemental forces in our life energy with their own vibrations and functions. They are essential to our health and well-being. Essentially, fear protects, anger defends, sadness releases, joy uplifts, compassion unites. Fear is close to the surface of our self, anger is rather deeper, sadness and joy are progressively more interior, and compassion emanates from our profound center. Each is a level and vibration of energy that needs to flow freely for us to be really engaged in the present.

A. Fear

Fear is a vitally useful emotion. It places you on the alert, catalyzes your senses, and heightens your awareness in the face of danger. Fear is your friend, the radar for your voyage through life. It is a basic instinct of human survival—physical, psychological, spiritual. We need to have an acute sense of what threatens our well-being. Sensitive antennae well-tuned to danger signals allow us to spot and deal with threats as they occur. Fear teaches us to pay attention to what's going on, and a well-honed sense of fear allows us to maintain dynamic equilibrium in a world that is inevitably insecure and unpredictable.

But fear's danger signals get muffled when we develop a pattern of denying and suppressing our fears. By not paying attention to specific fear signals, that energy gets diffused into a generalized paranoia, a perennial low-grade alarm fever that pervades our lives. And in my work, I find that virtually everyone is locked in fear; people are afraid of everything—losing their job, losing their lover, losing their life; they're afraid of success, afraid of being too happy, afraid of the truth, afraid of feeling, afraid of moving, of changing. As you become increasingly sensitive to the play of emotional energies, you can see (and feel in yourself) how unreleased fear tightens the throat, neck, and lower back, raises the shoulders, stiffens the jaw and contracts the forehead, immobilizes the pelvis and locks the knees. Fear writes its signature all over the body, but we're all so used to it we've become desensitized to the loud-and-clear message of our body language. And this pervasive fear simply compounds itself; it paralyzes our life energy, seizes up our feelings. We're so afraid of what we're going to lose, so painfully attached to what we have, that we numb ourselves into a living death to shield us from the pain of real living. By clinging to life as we have it, we deny ourselves a vibrant present and future.

What we need, then, is to free ourselves from our old, diffused, imploded anxieties so that we are able to fear what actually threatens our well-being. I remember one dramatic instance of fear imprisoning a life and then finally being released: There was a man in one of my workshops at Esalen who could speak but couldn't make any natural sounds. He was totally blocked and remained silent when the rest of the group moaned, grunted, hummed, and shouted. One day I was giving him a massage. While working on releasing the tension in his body, I noticed a big scar near his groin that was pulsating wildly. I laid my hand on it and asked him to breathe into my hand. He did. Suddenly, he threw back his head and let out a blood-curdling scream. People came running in from all sides, then froze in their places. After his eerie cry, he collapsed into unconsciousness, and the hushed crowd must have thought that he'd died. But I could feel him breathing. I covered him to keep him warm, and watched over him. When he regained consciousness, the pulsing sensation was gone. He told me that the pulsing near his groin had been going on for five years, since he was in Vietnam. There he'd had a bayonet shoved into his groin: he'd seen the thrust coming, had frozen in terror, and been unable to scream. Good soldiers don't scream. He'd ended up carrying that stifled scream around with him for years, and this cry of fear, buried alive inside him, had frozen not only his voice but all of his emotions.

We don't have to fear fear itself. We need not be embarrassed or immobilized by our fears. We need to give them appropriate attention and expression as they arise. Then the energy of fear is properly released. I work with actors a lot, and fear, of course, is a perennial issue. Stage fright, anxiety about performing well, remembering lines, etc., are perfectly appropriate. But what a good actor does is to transform that fear into its natural dynamic partner, excitement—and the resulting energy infuses the performance with an élan of risk, adventure, dancing on the edge. Fear properly channeled yields wide-awake engagement.

B. Anger

Anger is an integrity-protecting response to the invasion of your personal boundaries. It is "no" to a wrong, a violation. It draws lines and throws up barricades. Proper anger cuts like a knife through water. It is quick, clear, needs no explanation. It's the bared teeth of a bitch protecting her litter, the arched back and hiss of a cat threatened by a coyote. There's nothing cleaner, more effective than appropriate anger. Authentic anger is specific and justified, and its direct expression exposes impropriety and defends integrity in a way that benefits everyone.

My anger used to be locked up inside of me. I went to see Kastafayet, one of those impresarios of out-of-body experiences. It was appropriate to address him by saying, "How can I serve you?" So I did, and he answered, "You need to get angry with the whole world." I felt a shiver up my spine, and I must have looked lost because he added, "Don't worry. You deserve to be angry with everybody." And with that he closed his eyes and cut me off.

I was enraged. How dare he say I should be angry? What did he mean anyway? By the time I got home I was so furious I couldn't move my neck. It felt like a smoldering rod. I paced and stomped around my house. I finally constructed a tower of huge pillows and started pounding on them with all my might. On my knees, lifting my arms high above my head, gulping huge amounts of air and then letting it out as I smashed my hands into pillows. I vented my fury again and again until I fell in a heap, exhausted.

I kept this up for days. It seemed like I was being consumed by my anger, a lifetime of it spilling forth. Anger entered my voice even when I was trying to be tender and affectionate. I began practicing being angry, letting myself say and do things I'd always repressed. I stopped caring about whether what I said and did were appropriate or not. I felt totally off balance, possessed. I wrote angry letters that I didn't mail. And I danced and danced. I eventually thanked this mysterious character for instigating this venting of my stored-up anger. It was a big turning point in my life. And I guess what he meant was not that everybody deserved my anger, but that I needed to express all the anger I'd been harboring inside me.

Internalized, bottled-up anger is pandemic in our society and its consequences are catastrophic domestic violence, violent crime, all kinds of inappropriate aggression, war at all levels, despairing destructiveness. Anger is the most disallowed, unapproved of emotion in our society, and therefore the most repressed. The tell-tale body signs of repressed anger are visible all over: locked jaws, clenched fists, stiffened backs, jutting chins, raised voices, smoldering eyes. The evil seeds of imploded anger bloom in a thousand ways every day, destructive to others and ourselves. If we can only learn to be appropriately angry in the moment, protecting our personal territory against real invasion, anger would be a fitting response, an appropriate resolution of challenges, a treatment without negative side effects rather than a chronic condition whose impotence yields destruction. The authentic release of anger often yields a feeling of compassion, because you move from anger at the violation into a sympathetic appreciation of what caused the person to invade your boundaries. And anger itself can be an appropriate form of compassion.

C. Sadness

Sadness is the release, the emotional letdown when our expectations, our wishes are disappointed. The tension of expectation and intention is melted away. Sadness hurts because it involves letting go of what we're attached to— whether it be a good-night kiss, a gold medal, or a love affair—and living with loss. We are all familiar with the signs of sadness—the eyes are weary, the face droops, the back stoops, shoulders sag, arms hang, feet drag, and our speech gets sloppy and languid. Sadness is a kind of wilting all over.

Naturally, we fight sadness mightily. We want to be happy. The pursuit of happiness is a national right, a universal obsession. And we think that the obvious way to be happy, to have the lilt, sparkle, the high of happiness, is to avoid sadness. In fact, the opposite is true. It is only through accepting inevitable sadness that true joy is possible. For sadness is the healthy response to the blows to our expectations that are inevitable in living. We want things to stay the same, but life is change; we suffer hurt in the adjustment. We want people to treat us well, but we can't really control others (and still have vital relationships with them). Disappointments can't be avoided.

Sadness, then, connects you to the core of your vulnerability and the primal attachments that constitute the web of your experience. It is an energy of release, a thunderstorm that breaks the tension and clears the air. It is a dissolving dance, a chaotic vibration at the cellular level, engendering a healing catharsis vital to your being's fluidity and resilience. Sadness is the transforming medium in our lives that allows us to meld our rigidity, our longing for security, stability, and assurance, with the inevitability of change and the need for growth. The challenge is to accept our inescapable vulnerability and to embrace the experience of sadness when it comes, as the release necessary to living healthily with change. We should never scale back our expectations or our real wants in order to escape the pain of not getting them; rather, we should go for just what we want, what we need, what really satisfies, and literally and figuratively sing the blues if we don't get it. Avoiding sadness results in a superficial happiness, a kind of life laugh-track that masks an all-too-apparent undercurrent of depression: it is the permanent station to which so many lives are tuned. Thoreau's observation remains truer than ever: most people lead lives of quiet desperation; that is, lives of masked fear, anger, and sadness. And it is the avoidance of these emotions that returns to haunt our lives, especially the flight from sadness.

As everyone knows, children cry a lot. They go hellbent for something, get stymied, and scream in protest. Life is always disappointing them, and they let loose with their unhappiness. And when the crying's done, it's over; there's no lingering trail of depression. But children are soon taught that crying and sadness are to be avoided, if possible, and not something good: "Now there, don't cry....", "What's wrong with you?"; "Don't be a sissy"; "Don't be a baby!"

It's so easy to fall into the trap of trying to protect our children from inevitable disappointments. I remember taking my son out to a restaurant in Big Sur one night to get him some hot chocolate, which he loved as a kid. When we got there, they said that they were out of hot chocolate. I was outraged and hurt. They always had hot chocolate. They had to have it. Jonathan loved hot chocolate. He had to have it. I went on and on. Well, don't you have some chocolate syrup and some milk? Don't you have some sort of instant? I badgered them about every possible way that they could produce this hot chocolate. Jonathan watched all this with growing alarm and embarrassment. Finally he said, "Don't worry about it, Mom. I'm only disappointed."

How much do we shield ourselves and our children from disappointment, from pain, from sadness? We have to realize that we are just shielding ourselves and them from the healthful processes of living. And the protecting never really works anyway. I know a very successful businessman who has daily triumphs in his work, a great family, and seems to deny himself none of life's pleasures. But every time I meet him an aura of sadness fills the room, a heaviness envelops him. He sucks life right out of the air. The fact is that he is desperately afraid of admitting failure or pain or disappointment; he maintains a seamless cloak of well-being, which is in fact a heavy veil of depression that colors everything he does, turning all the gold of his life into dross. But he's afraid to admit his suffering to himself or anyone, because he's aware at some level that the whole house of cards would then come tumbling down. If he let himself cry, who knows what floodgates would open up? But meanwhile his dammed-up emotions leave his life stagnant. Similarly, we all know party animals and jokesters whose constant pursuit of fun is a transparent flight from ennui.

Sadness signals the need to release an attachment. It is a symptom from the heart that warrants heeding. And if we learn to sing the blues of our life, we'll discover soon enough that expressing sadness inevitably yields joy. When life disappoints us and runs counter to our fondest wishes, sadness is the authentic response, whose cleansing energy allows the free flow of the rest of our feelings.

D. Joy

Joy is the expansive energy of dynamic well-being. It uplifts, energizes, makes our eyes shine, gives a lilt to our step, light to our whole being. Joy is naturally generous and relaxed and open. It comes when our emotional energy flows freely in a dynamic of appropriate responses to our experiences. Many of us experience the natural high that comes in running or dancing or other physical activities, when you reach the point where your body is moving wholly, naturally, unforced—like an animal's—with everything working and in sync.

Such joy comes, of course, only when the other emotions of fear, anger, or sadness flow. We generally think that we know what joy is, but we really don't. We sometimes confuse it with a society-sanctioned "happiness," which puts a kind of perennial happy face on all our doings. But such happiness is transitory and illusory: scratch the surface and you'll find just the opposite. I remember once having lunch in New York with a hip young man from Chicago and a lady friend of mine. Over drink after drink, cigarette after cigarette, she was going on and on about all the things she was doing; what a wonderful, perfect person her husband was, how great their relationship was. After taking this all in, this amazing young man leaned close to her and gently said, "Say, baby, you unhappy?" I remember her expression as if it were yesterday: a hard truth had slapped her across the face. "Unhappy," she whispered, looking at him and then me in a stunned stupor. Her body seemed to sink back into the chair. "Yes, I am unhappy. I can't believe it, I'm very unhappy!" And she started to laugh and cry. "How simple. How could I not know that I'm unhappy?" she softly asked herself. Although she had been denying it to herself and shielding it from everyone else, she really was miserable. Perhaps we all knew it intuitively, but couldn't bring ourselves to think it or say it.

And she was married to a truly wonderful person and it should have been great. But it wasn't.

Most people pretend to be happy, because that's what you're supposed to be; it's the acceptable state of being. But true contentment is pretty rare. I know that when for years I denied my fear, anger, sadness, which is what most of us do, I wasn't happy. People around me thought that I was happy, because I was fun and funny. But my funniness was a self-deprecating way of masking the pain. I was in constant, desperate pursuit of something, someone to fill the black hole I felt inside. Joy doesn't come through fixes.

When joy does come, it should be celebrated, although many of us are embarrassed by spontaneous bursts of elation. It's not that we think there's something wrong with being joyful, but that we have a notion it's not cool or sophisticated to be *too* joyful, or too openly emotional. We're often as uncomfortable about having hearts as we are about having bodies.

My early experiences of pure, untrammeled joy came wholly by accident, without trying. Those experiences were the birth of my son and the natural ecstasy of nursing him. The birthing and nurturing of a child are prime examples of that pure rhythm of giving and receiving, being totally in the moment, feeling it completely right—the essence of joy. If you talk to mothers about this, especially new ones, you'll experience the glow of ready recognition.

Joy is as vital to us as the other emotions. It is healing, restorative, encouraging of the way we're meant to be. We've heard a lot recently, from Norman Cousins and others, about the healing power of humor. It's true that humor is a vital way of unburdening us from pressures and expectations, cutting things down to size, and giving us delight in experiencing the moment. Humor brings a vital message of the essential arbitrariness, precariousness, and absurdity of life, and yet here we are, despite this, able to live and be. There's something holy about laughing with Robin Williams or Lily Tomlin when they're cooking and they get things just right. A sometimes-wise friend of mine once said that he didn't trust the truth of any religion or any religious teacher that didn't have a sense of humor. The reason is simple: humor allows us to see things straight, acknowledging just how little we know, how fallible we are, how far from perfect or finished. Humor releases us into this realization for a moment. It also frees us from solemn attachments, and it is this freedom from attachments, to be without wanting or regretting, that constitutes real joy.

It's only in my later life that I'm becoming more and more happy day in and day out. Because I'm not so afraid of my fear, anger, sadness, or my attachments, my fixed expectations are fewer. I go more and more with the energy as it comes. Joy is less and less a momentary rush, and more of an undercurrent, the accompanying music singing through my days. And it is out of this dynamic contentment that my teaching can come—energetically giving people just what they need in the moment. For when you're joyous, you can be spontaneous; you're not forever fleeing the feared pain of the moment by always wanting to be somewhere else, in some altered state, in some bygone past or not-yet future.

E. Compassion

Compassion comes as the fruit of fear, anger, sadness, and joy. When you know these emotions in your everyday life, you can then empathize with them in others' lives and begin to give people precisely what they really need. Compassion is not always a hug; sometimes it's like a slap in the face. It involves being able to feel what another is feeling while remaining sufficiently detached to know what is needed and then to respond appropriately. You might feel someone's pain, joy, fear, but it's not yours; rather, the *emo-*

tion connects you to them. If you're truly compassionate, when someone is afraid it doesn't make you afraid, but allows you to feel and relate to their fear. You can genuinely empathize because you're free of muddling projections of your own.

When I started working with actors in the early seventies, I asked them to express the five emotions. I was amazed at what I discovered. Here I was working with the most expressive part of the population, professional actors, and all of them came up with the same limited range of clichéd expressions of each emotion. I saw then and there that we were totally cut off from our true emotional life; even these professionals had succumbed to the pop TV vocabulary of emotion. The hardest of all for them to express was compassion. They all made some tear-choking outstretching of the hand to some presumed unfortunate.

But compassion involves recognizing the emotions operating in others and responding appropriately to what's going on. Compassion is a chameleon: it can wear the face of fear, anger, sadness, joy, or even dispassion, depending on what's needed at the time. The compassionate Buddha has a smile in one eye and a tear in the other, and our Buddha mission is to lead people to true freedom, not to hold their hand and tell them that everything is going to be all right. In teaching, compassion means doing whatever needs to be done to get to the next phase.

The common misconception, of course, is that compassion means feeling sorry for other people. Such feelings generally amount to nothing more than sentimentality: feeling sympathy without having any real intention of doing anything about the other person's situation; it's a cheap out, suffused with the illusion of being a good, caring person. We all like to think of ourselves as compassionate, nice people. But, of course, many of us don't know what being compassionate really means. I remember once doing a workshop on the emotions in which I divided up the

participants by asking people to go into five different theater groups, one for each of the five emotions. About half of
them flocked into compassion, and nobody went into anger. So I said, "OK, all those in compassion will be the
anger group instead." Well, there was a great hue and cry,
people screaming at the top of their lungs, "I'm not angry!
I don't belong in the anger group." Others sulked in resentment. In short order, these people discovered the paradox of
their response: they had just done the anger theater piece,
albeit unconsciously.

Sometimes compassion means *not* going along with
someone's emotions. Once during a massage course I was
teaching, a woman lay on the massage table and began to
cry hysterically. Her partner and those around her were
repelled. They stood back, not knowing what to do, confusion and pain racking their faces. Something in her tone,
the vibration of her whole energy, kept me at a distance.
The others, unable to resist her, grudgingly moved toward
her and tried to comfort her, or at least stop her crying,
with a muddled mixture of half-hearted reassurances and
random stroking. They looked to me helplessly, and I smiled
softly. Later they asked me why I'd done nothing and why
they'd felt so cold, so unmoved by her pain. "It's simple," I
said, "it wasn't real. She was manipulating you, and deep
down you knew it. But her will was stronger."

This happens to us often in life. In my experience,
when someone is feeling real pain, we feel an inclination
to respond on an equally real basis. I remember another
time at Esalen when, young and scared, I participated in
one of my first encounter groups. We were all sitting in a
tub at the baths, and one woman started crying loudly and
forcefully. She was apparently mourning for her husband
who had died seven years before. She was down in the
water, while the rest of us were sitting around the sides of
the tub. The leader asked her to go around and ask each of
us for our support. She did. One by one the members of the

group got down into the water and hugged her. Her tears continued to tumble forth. I was the last one to be asked. As she sat before me, I couldn't escape the idea that she was wallowing in self-pity. She asked me for my support, and I heard myself say, "Of course, I support you. But I want you to come up here, since I don't feel right about getting down there with you. I can only support you by you coming up here." The others judged me harsh and cold. Yet I knew she knew I knew. I'd been given a glimpse of her soul, and she knew it. She was ready to move on.

In both these cases, my sense of compassion was to let a person be. Feeling the absence of my abetting their histrionics was what they really needed rather than the natural gesture of holding their hand; it was what they needed to move on to the next square. In other situations, however, it is precisely a hug, or comfort, or company that people need to get them to move on. A compassionate person is always directing the energy toward movement and change. If the widow had had her lowest level given unqualified support, how would she ever move past her grief?

Compassion means giving someone what they need, which is not always what they want. For example, imagine you're with a man who is sad. It is not compassionate to try to talk him out of it, to pretend that everything is perfectly OK. If it were, he wouldn't be sad. Rather it is best to feel the core of that sadness, to realize and affirm that he has to move through it, not around or above it, and maybe even to cry with him.

Not only does false compassion surround us—sentimental feelings devoid of ethical obligation—but so does hardheartedness or even heartlessness; people are too numb or emotionally wounded to see and respond to others. One day I took a break from a workshop I was teaching in New York and went across the street to Dunbar's cafeteria, a local hangout for the over-sixty crowd living on fixed incomes. I was in line behind a sweet old man, who carefully selected his mashed potatoes, peas, cottage cheese, and jello; it seemed his major daily ritual out in the world. When he got to the cashier he tried several times to engage her in conversation, saying things like, "Well, you'd think I'd come up with a new menu one day. But nope, the same old things. I guess I must like it, which is what counts, right?" The cashier just stared straight ahead, stone-faced: "That'll be $5.49. Next." The man looked utterly crushed as he shuffled to a table where he sat down all alone. All he wanted was a little contact, a smile, a little bit of recognition. But she'd sealed off her vulnerability, somehow decided that it would deplete her to give anything of herself. But the fact is that it clearly took more energy for her to maintain her stony indifference than it would have to become emotionally engaged with "all the lonely people" she encountered every day.

Many of us have the idea that emotional energy is like fuel—if you spend it, use it, give it away, then you'll have less. This energy, however, is not a commodity that becomes depleted with use. Like the blood in our circulatory system, it needs to flow, to be used up, and will replenish itself and keep us healthy. Hoarding emotional energy, damming it up, saves nothing; it only causes damage, and is ultimately suicidal. So not only was the cashier denying this man reassurance that he wasn't alone, some human warmth that might make his day worth living, but she was obviously making herself into an emotional corpse, a dead stump of a person. In fact, recent psychological studies show that there are physiological benefits to doing acts of kindness; the body gets a natural lift and release from its heartfelt responses.

Of course, not all pleas for attention merit a response. I once had a woman in a workshop who interrupted everything I did. It was her obsession to constantly divert attention to herself. Once the pattern had become clear, I made a circle of the group and asked her to stand in the center of it. I said gently, "Now you have our undivided attention." She burst into tears.

Often compassion involves sharing someone else's emotion. The best thing to do with an angry child is not to try to turn off the anger, to push it down, to insist that the anger be controlled; rather, it is best to give the anger permission, to affirm it. Maybe you can get down with the child and do an angry, stomping, monster dance together. It is so vital for us to help our mates, lovers, children, and friends in letting their emotions breathe and find apt expression. Compassion supports other people in entering into and releasing their authentic feelings, and exposes phony emotions.

In many families, some emotions are OK and others are not. In my husband's, anger was natural and its expression sanctioned; he and his family felt easy about letting their anger out. In my family, anger was forbidden, but sadness was accepted. So I had to learn not to become scared by my husband's anger, and he had to learn not to get angry at my sadness. We had to teach and affirm the alien emotion to each other so that he could accept sadness and I could experience anger. This sort of exchange is vitally necessary if a really healthy, alive, multidimensional relationship is going to exist. The fact that this exchange doesn't happen is one of the reasons why so many relationships become desiccated and fail. The life blood of a relationship becomes blocked by clots of repression and denial, and our creative, life-building energy is absorbed by exhausting strategies of avoidance.

From one perspective, compassion is the absence of emotion. That is, you are so free of your emotional past that you are open to the truth of others' feelings. In that sense, compassion is an empty vessel. If you're full of your own fear, you can't respond to another's. Only when you begin to be a finely tuned emotional instrument can you play the lyric and melody of other's feelings. And if you truly feel another's feeling, then you'll respond appropriately, rather than through a distorted filter of unresolved fear, or anger, or sadness. Compassion may be said to be the absence of emotion from which all emotion flows, just as dynamic stillness is the source of all movement.

2. THE SONG OF THE HEART

Singing and songs are an integral part of every culture. In songs, we express our fury and pain, our joys and sorrows, our caring and concerns. In traditional societies—African tribes, Scottish villages, Native American communities—everyone sings; the songs are for everyone. But for contemporary, secular people, singing has become a specialty: professional singers sing and the rest of us listen. Still, for reasons we are barely conscious of, songs remain a vital part of living: musical cultures flourish—rock, opera, jazz; people are listening, night and day, in their cars and homes, to songs. Once you think about it a little, it's clear that we're dependent on songs and singers to supply us with almost constant emotional energy. Our hunger for songs and our adulation of singers signal our desperate need to share in the raw expression of emotions. Songs are one of the few areas in which the exploration of the full range of emotions is publicly sanctioned and wholly accepted, even in a mass culture where the tendency is to repress real feelings or replace them with pale or cheap imitations.

If the magic of the singer shows us how to explore the full range of the emotions, then one thing we can do to catalyze our emotions is to discover the singer within ourselves. An easy way to do this initially is just to sing along with singers you like and with whom you identify. Find songs that connect you to your fear, anger, sadness, joy, and compassion.

Feelings get stuck in the throat. We get choked up with sadness, constricted with fear. But if we could full-throatedly wail our grief as mourning Spanish peasant women do, or shout our joy like celebrating Zulus, we'd begin to feel the pulse of pure emotion once more. Singing is a simple, immediate way to free the flow of feeling and to keep it flowing day after day. Awaken the singer in you, just as you did the dancer, not with the aim of becoming a professional singer, but just to become a fully functioning human being.

If you're afraid to sing, hum. Hum freely and deeply, letting the sound well up from your belly. Feel it vibrate in your body. Hum from your chest, your heart. Finally, move the hum up to its highest pitch, letting it vibrate through your head.

Then you can let your hum turn into a melody. Surrender to your song, follow it into your heart, and you'll feel your soul stir. Sometimes words come, sometimes they don't. It doesn't matter. Just let the sound come from your gut, and let it move your body. This is the voice of your heart.

Your voice takes you to your heart. So can dancing the rhythms. Mobilizing the sound within, and moving your body—both catalyze emotions. Singing and dancing put you in direct touch with how you are feeling in the moment. They also release old feelings, energy that has been trapped in your body with nowhere to go. Let it go—both the present energy coursing through you and the past energy that's gotten bottled up. Sing and dance how you feel.

Discovering your voice and your capacity for the feeling range of songs is a readily available and very secure and private way to discover firsthand the contour and feel of the basic emotions. Another way is to do the rhythms as a means of expressing a specific emotion. Use the flowing rhythms to feel your fear; use staccato to feel and express anger, chaos for sadness, lyrical for joy, stillness for compassion. The rhythms catalyze each emotion and each stage of each emotion.

Each feeling not only has a home rhythm, but each feeling moves through all the rhythms as well. You can dance out your anger, expressing it in the waves of the rhythms: first in flowing movements, controlling, containing, breathing into your resentment, exaggerating it; letting the anger build until it breaks out in bold, quick staccato moves—anger's quintessential expression; then overflowing into a chaotic fury, wildly gesticulating your rage— kicking, throwing imaginary things, losing all control; ultimately, fury spends itself and you surrender to the far edge of your anger, into lyric flippancy; and then settling into a still attitude of calm defiance, moving from one calm, defiant posture to the next.

In dancing and singing, you are discovering and releasing the energy of the emotion, allowing it to flow through and out of you. The result, for instance, of dancing through the rhythms of anger is to reach a calm, grounded position from which to effectively and appropriately deal with the source of your anger, rather than just chaotically erupting, or simmering until you explode, or jabbing away with slights and insults like an overmatched boxer. At the same time, you become familiar with the emotion and begin to feel natural with its phases and expressions.

When emotions come, as they inevitably will, dance them, move them, and confront people, situations, and challenges from a point of centered stillness. Blocked emotions end up exploding or festering and have much more impact than they should.

Of course, the simple injunction to express your emotions is not enough. The vital, healing work of moving our emotions requires discovering and then releasing our true feelings. Singing and moving emotions are good ways to start, and good everyday practices once you're underway.

But as most of us start this shamanic work with a checkered emotional history, it is important to understand our past. Generally, we're taught early on to repress or deny our feelings in various ways: "Don't cry, it's all right." "Don't talk to me that way!" "You're out of control." "Come on, don't be a sissy." We quickly learn that we should keep things buttoned down as much as possible and operate in a narrow emotional range, putting on a happy face and exhibiting a universal willingness to please. But repressed emotions just go underground, build up, and become distorted, with the result that their eventual expression is often inappropriate and out of sync.

3. Discovering Your Emotional Self

Most of us think that we know a lot about our emotional lives. We've all been fearful, angry, sad, joyous, caring. But how familiar are we with our true feelings? If you're feeling sad, depressed, or dispirited, is sadness the real core emotion or is it the self-inflicted wound caused by repressed anger? A humorous response to a bizarre situation is to say, "I didn't know whether to laugh or cry"; but don't we often find ourselves in situations where we don't know what we feel? We're so conditioned into thinking about what we *should* feel, or our emotional faculties are so dampened and distorted, that many of us are emotionally confused to the point that we sometimes don't know whether to laugh or cry.

It is vital to discover our emotional selves. As you moved your body to experience the energy of your feelings, you can use your mind to explore them. You can say to yourself: "It scares me...." or "It pisses me off...." or "It makes me sad...." Whichever one you choose, use the phrase to trigger a stream of consciousness monologue. You can think it to yourself, internally. You can say it out loud. You can do it on paper. You can do it in flowing, staccato, or from a deep, centered stillness.

You have the power to become aware of the emotions that are coursing through your life—to know the contours, the patterns, the dynamics of your feelings, what they focus on and how they move. And for those of us who are basically afraid of our emotions, because we've learned early on that they're messy, disruptive, nonlinear, etc. (like life!), such exercises are a nonthreatening way to make friends of our feelings, to not be so thrown by them. The aim is to be gradually more aware and at home with our whole emotional range, so that we know what we really feel, and are able to express those feelings appropriately and directly. Putting the emotions or an emotion through the rhythms, as well as this inventory of feelings, makes us familiar with them as basic components of our instinctual life energy and lets us gradually become masters of their appropriate expression.

Since our feelings are generally locked into distorted patterns of masked and inappropriate responses, now excessively muted and now excessively explosive, just expressing our feelings isn't enough. It's not that we lack for emotional expression: there's plenty of that around. The papers are full of stories of the emotional weather—murders, rapes, terrifying experiences, people doing things for other people, fun parties, thrilling victories. And in our personal lives, we see and sense feelings being expressed all the time. But often what we regularly encounter are not true expressions of feeling, pure emotions, but distorted ones: rapes are not expressions of lust, but of anger and hatred; we get angry at someone and take out the anger on ourselves by self-destructively smoking a pack of cigarettes or getting drunk or stuffing ourselves with junk food; we're the life of the party, talking a blue streak and dancing up a storm, because we're afraid of being alone, of acknowledging our loneliness.

Unacknowledged fear is, in fact, at the root of many of our lives. I discovered the pervasiveness of fear early on in teaching movement and massage, since fear inhibits movement and keeps us literally uptight. And I still find in all my work how filled with fear, how numbed with unnamed terror people are. We live in fear of our emotions and develop all kinds of strategies and coping mechanisms to avoid experiencing them. If we just began to know and express our fears, it would be a great start. I've seen the healing power of the honest acknowledgment of fears in working with individuals and groups, and myself.

Once, in a workshop, I asked each person in the group to honestly and spontaneously complete the sentence, "I feel scared when...." The first person bravely let loose a deep fear. And as each person voiced his fears, the raw honesty and scary range of fear grew so that everyone felt that they couldn't hedge, couldn't hide behind lies or illusions. The honest expression of feelings itself engendered courage, eloquence, and clarity.

That night in my dreams I relived a traumatic event that had occurred when my son was nine months old. I heard him cry for his early morning feeding, but he only cried once. It was 5:00 A.M., and I almost didn't get up. He was laying in his crib, grey and still. I froze in terror, then managed to call the doctor. I described my baby's condition, and the doctor, sounding grave and urgent, suggested I pick him up and come immediately to the emergency hospital. He said, "Where are you?" When I said, "Big Sur," he swore, "Shit!" I'll never forget the sound of the silence that followed.

It was an hour and a half drive to the hospital on a winding highway with hairpin curves and mountainous cliffs that I'd lost several friends to. All the way I did mouth-to-mouth resuscitation as a friend drove. Occasional cars wouldn't let us pass. My baby was turning blue, and I was terrified.

We got to the hospital. Everything happened with the staccato energy of a movie on fast forward. The doctor was grim-faced. I watched him put a huge needle in my son's spine; my son didn't even wince. They made me leave the room.

I paced. I smoked. I prayed. I begged. I pushed back my tears. I have never been this afraid again. Finally a nurse came and got me. It'd been about six hours since I had arrived. I followed her into a room where my baby lay smiling and gurgling in his crib. "He's hungry," she said. The doctor nodded his head. Nobody knew what had happened, but whatever it was, it was now over. Probably an aborted crib death, a mystery.

I swelled with joy. But I forgot something. I forgot to scream, to cry my heart out, to release the tension that lived on long after, haunting my mind with the terror of loss.

I woke up the next morning, after this dream, and knew why this terror had stalked me for so long. So I danced it out. I shared my experience with the group. I let it go.

It was at times like these I discovered that the pure expression of feelings is magical and healing. And gradually it happens not just in workshops, but as a force in your life.

4. THE PULSING OF LOVE

The expression and release of our true feelings constitute the essence of loving. The boy-girl, romantic notion of love is but a small part of the picture; to think of that as the whole story of love is like reducing a whole biography to one episode, a jigsaw puzzle to one piece, a musical score to one passage. Love is essentially the primal energy of all our emotions flowing, of really feeling and responding moment by moment, situation by situation. Saint Augustine once summed up all of Christian teaching about how to live as "Love and do what you will." It seemed a dangerously libertine thing to say, especially for a puritanical cleric like Augustine. But if love is the healthy functioning of our whole emotional system, then when we love we will naturally end up doing the right thing. Love is not a mood, but a dynamic way of being. Love's realm is not the soap opera portion of our lives, but the whole of our interchange with ourselves and others. Living love, living powerfully through love, involves getting into the rhythm of the basic life energies that sustain us.

Obviously love—and the movement of the emotions of fear, anger, sadness, joy, compassion—is on the borderline between the body and the mind. Feelings are both physical and mental: they manifest in our bodies, and most of our thoughts focus on or at least are colored by our feelings. The power of loving clearly requires a mental component as well, a self-knowledge that is empowering.

Most of us arrive at the stage in life where we're expected and expect to develop and sustain loving relationships—with a mate, with our children, with our families, friends, community. But often we are as incompetent and unprepared for this as children expected to sing opera. We don't have the experience, the range, the training, the creative freedom, to carry a tune let alone to sing an aria. All the world loves a lover, but hardly anyone learns how to become one. So in the next chapter on freeing the mind, we explore the stages of life through which we become mature lovers.

THREE
Emptying the Mind
THE POWER OF KNOWING

The perfect man
uses his mind
as a mirror.
It grasps nothing.
It regrets nothing.
It receives but
does not keep.

Chuang Tzu[6]

The third shamanic task is to empty the mind to experience the power of true knowing. Knowing what? The true self—whoever that is. But I can guarantee you that your true self is somebody well worth knowing. "Know thyself," the ancient oracle counseled Socrates. Empty the mind of all its chatter and see what's there. This is the work of self-knowledge: to uncover your authentic self.

This self is the part of us that functions on instincts. The part of us that tends to be hidden. It gets buried in personal history, in our unique experience of the life cycles of birth, childhood, puberty, maturity, and death. By looking back at our personal history (from the perspective of the life cycles), we can unearth who we are and why we are not fully the person we're meant to be. We need to reclaim the instincts that are vital to fully being who we uniquely are.

The basic instincts of being human come to us through our sacred teachers of each life cycle. Each life cycle has its main catalyst and its teaching. At each stage of our lives there are essential experiences we need to have, truths we need to learn, things that need to happen.

Often these crucial instinct-building events don't occur. Instead, we acquire patterns that bind rather than free us, that uproot rather than ground us. It's our present challenge to change the patterns that hold our true self in check. But we must first become aware of them, and that requires unraveling the mystery of how we've come to be the way we are.

Life itself, through its stages of development, is the path to enlightenment. All we have to do is to live it, not fight it, control it, or resist it. A mysterious game life is: the only way to win is to surrender.

It would be wonderful if we were all perfect, enlightened people, rooted in the practice of sacred ways, traditional rites of passage, empowering visions and teachings. But we're not, and the result is a lot of suffering as we improvise our growth and heal the wounds of ignorance and misdirection. All we can do is to turn that suffering into awareness, that awareness into art. Survival art. We dance. We sing. And now we write.

This chapter is about digging up memories by their roots. It is the task of the writer, the empowering archetype for the shamanic freeing of the mind. The writer digs deep to find the crucial moments that give a life its character and finds the connecting links that free one to speak with one's own distinctive voice.

Personal writing is healing. We need to liberate the writer within from the prison of hollow noise we live in.

We need to write to find out what's true for us. We need to find out what we know and what we don't know. We need to open our minds.

1. DISCOVERING YOUR OWN MIND

The mind is a camera: it creates, perceives, and records reality. Its depth is unfathomable; its breadth unimaginable; its energy boundless. We rarely tap into the core of our reality with innocence—the key to magic. We don't want magic. We want everything to be safe, predictable, even boring, and that's why we routinely operate at the level of the superficial—the calculating, judging mind, the mind as master sergeant, fitting everything into set routines. This mind is cramped, cluttered, and thinks it knows everything. For it, nothing is new, fresh, or mysterious.

However, we do sense there's another dimension and we long for it. We experience, however fleetingly, an open and perceiving self, a level of mind that is prior to and independent from our cut-and-dried, know-it-all mind. I call it the intuitive mind, which is lithe, receptive, responsive, present in the moment. This attentive mind is like a well-trained athlete, a disciplined dancer, a chess or aikido master—a mind that has all the subtleness, flexibility, range, and appropriated knowledge to deal with every person and every situation in a totally focused and appropriate way. This mind comes naturally to us; it's our spontaneous way of thinking. But it's usually buried early by training and teaching that educate us out of our natural, attentive way of being in the world, and into an artificial way of being that fits us in with the neuroses and agendas of our society. Mostly the miseducation is unwittingly done by people who are themselves misdirected and in pain. There's no point in blaming others, just corrective work to do.

Thus, we need to empty the junkyard level of our mind so that we can liberate its true potential for real knowledge—personal, self-appropriated wisdom. Achieving mindfulness, as the Buddhists call it, is a lifelong task that involves both thinking and unthinking, emptying the mind of what doesn't matter and filling it with what does. Our heads are so filled with thoughts that we can't think here and now. We have a constant mental Walkman going on, playing the same obsessive tapes of questions, opinions, worries, precautions: who to be, what to say, how to do, when to come, when to go; what they think, what they'll do, how that happened, what to watch out for, and so on, and so on. We don't have an animal's, or a master's freedom to move on instinct: we either plan every move or we get caught up in someone else's agenda. We think before we speak, before we act, before we breathe. We think and think. We think too much. Our calculating mind is like an assembly line running night and day packaging our experience. We need to turn the damn thing off in order to figure out what's really going on in our lives.

When my son was three years old, he astonished me one morning when I overheard him talking to a grown-up friend of ours. This man was completely out of touch with his heart, unable to see anyone but himself. This particular morning he was mindlessly lecturing my small son, who abruptly stopped eating his cereal, stared at this hollow man, and blurted out: "Words, words, words—is that all you have?"

The mind doesn't turn off. It stays busy manipulating, remembering, projecting. All this combining and recombining is what most people nowadays regard as the mind, and they call this empirical, measurable dimension of mind "intelligence." This calculating mind never rests, even in sleep, except to the degree that we can focus our consciousness into the deeper center of mindfulness—the intuitive, receptive dimension of our thinking selves. The philosopher Ludwig Wittgenstein was addicted to simple-minded American movies, especially musicals, which he would watch from the front row in empty theaters. When asked why he did this, he said, "It's the only way I can stop my mind."

For me, the best way to still my mind is to move my body. And a mind emptied of busyness (the "business" that preoccupies most of our lives) and redirected into the natural rhythms of our body and heart has immeasurable power, an unlimited capacity for wisdom.

The mind is the bridge between the higher and lower dimensions of our selves. It leads toward unconsciousness or toward enlightenment, living in the dark or in the light. We can use the mind to recognize and to heal our own psychic wounds. Or we can allow it to go on automatic pilot and drift across the surface of reality. Nobody can make the choice but you and me.

2. THE FIVE SACRED TEACHERS ON THE JOURNEY OF LIFE

Life is a journey. Its route is essentially the same for everyone, even though we start in different settings and with different baggage.

Everybody is born, everybody dies, and most go the full cycle from birth through childhood, puberty, and maturity to death.

To be wise we have to know just how our psyches were formed, how they were wounded, how they were blessed. And how to heal what hampers our full being. Our wounds and our blessings are the raw material of our enlightenment. The more consciously we process them, the closer we move to fulfilling our psychic potential.

The answers lie in our own personal histories. Each of our life stories unfolds in natural cycles, each cycle having its natural teacher: our birth/our mother; our childhood/our father; our puberty/our self; our maturity/our society; our seniority/our universe. Our unique story line shows our particular relationships to all of these and to the other people in our life.

From the five sacred teachers—mother; father; self; society; universe—we learn all the personal wisdom we need to know. These guides on our life journey, whether they or we know it or not, are crucial to our personal development. They are our mirrors. It is from them that we learn our basic life instincts, our spontaneous ways of being, of responding to life's challenges. Many of us are walking around without the healthy instincts with which to live a rich life. We are like an adult child thrown into a hockey game, not knowing how to move, let alone how to defend against attacks or mount offensives. We're not really in the game at all, but get clobbered coming and going nonetheless. In a sense, we're all victims of psychic AIDS, since our natural self-protective and self-healing, wholeness-making instincts are weak. So much of the suffering and grief in our personal lives, our cities, our country, our world, are rooted in people's radical insufficiency in the basic instincts that constitute whole and natural human living.

Everywhere I look I see wounded children struggling to exist. How did we all become so wounded? Modern history tells us all about the world wars, Korea, Vietnam, etc., but who tells us about the child wars we've all been through, fighting for our freedom?

We've all been through the child wars. My teacher Oscar Ichazo taught me how mother and father, in particular, shape our psyches during this struggle, and he showed me how to stop the world and watch myself move. In these movements I saw the same patterns repeating over and over.

He named these patterns, tracing them back to zero. He led me back to the Garden of Eden and asked, "Do you really want to leave?" In his vision, I saw the simple truth of my life. My wounds. My blessings. My point of view. My story. This knowledge freed me to keep moving toward the self I'd buried, to reclaim my instincts.

To reclaim our natural instincts for self-preservation and self-enhancement, the mind has to be liberated from the past and the future so it can be more fully present, spontaneous, magical, intuitive. You've got to know the past to erase it. And erasing the past erases the future, leaving space for something real to happen. Something new.

Our teachers—mother, father, self, society, and universe—are naturally empowered to give us the instincts we need to function appropriately in an ever-changing world. We are all called upon to be as resourceful as an Indian tracker, a street-smart saint, a one-room school teacher, an Eskimo or a Bedouin. It is truly a matter of life or death to discover what our own life teachers succeeded and failed in giving us. What instincts, what life skills did we receive that liberate the mind, and what restrictive conditioning did we get that programs us to be less than we are? If you have been lucky and received the basic knowledge and wisdom, feelings and energy appropriate to each stage, then you probably handle life's day-to-day challenges with grace and alacrity. What to many is a battle, a struggle, is to you a dance, a game. But how many people do you see really having fun, dancing through life?

If you didn't get what you needed, things don't come naturally. You have to think about everything. When knowing is instinctual, then deliberation, doubt, hesitation, etc., are unnecessary and inappropriate.

Like the immune system, our vital instincts are inborn response patterns. But they must be catalyzed by our sacred teachers. They're switches to be turned on. The evolution of our instinctual system proceeds through the life cycles. In each, the interaction with the teacher should awaken an instinct, a natural, spontaneous way of being.

We are, for the most part, far away from any sense of the sacred roles we play in each other's lives. Mothering is regarded as childcare, a job others can do equally well or better. Fathering means being the often absent chief executive and financial officer of the family. The self-determination of our adolescence is routinely dominated by parental and societal pressures. Maturity is hard to achieve in an immature culture. And the final cycle of life, its consummation in death, is much more disparaged and avoided than appreciated and embraced.

We are not getting what we need. Look at the walking wounded in your neighborhood, your family, your mirror. Support for the crucial tasks of each stage in the life cycle, common in so-called primitive tribes and peasant village life, is much more difficult and unappreciated in modern society. We no longer honor life's whole sacred journey. Our rituals are empty; they mean nothing. They no longer empower us for the psychic tasks we need to undertake. What are our rituals for birth, for childhood, for puberty, for maturity, for death? Do we have any that are really transforming? I think not. That's why we need to practice a creative, contemporary shamanism suited to our turbulent, tenuous times.

Our mothers catalyze our nurturing instincts. Our fathers our fellowship instincts. We catalyze our own internal instincts, and society—the other people and social institutions in our lives—catalyzes our social instincts. Contemplation and wisdom about our oneness with the universe brings out our instinct for the eternal, what really lasts and matters. This final instinct comes only with the integration of the prior four in the psyche. And only when we connect with the eternal can we die in fullness and peace.

Birth. Childhood. Puberty. Maturity. Death. The dance of life in five movements. Life is a work-in-progress, performance art, ritual theater, an epic poem, and we're not called to be only spectators and listeners, but the artists of our own stories, the creator of our own lives. What role are you playing in your life? Why? Do you have a choice? Yes!

You can direct and star in your own movie, or you can play bit parts in other people's productions. You can choose to be fully aware or to play dumb. I play lots of roles. A vital one is student: Life is my master. Teachers come and go. In each step of the process, a teacher is to be met, lessons learned, relationships completed, instincts appropriated. What's the story of your teachers, your pilgrim's progress? It's time to get it down in writing.

3. WRITING YOUR STORY

When you dance, you ritualize how you move. When you sing, you ritualize how you feel. In writing, you ritualize how you think.

I'll be outlining my angle on the basic cycles of life. But my words will be empty unless you fill in the picture with your own distinctive experience. What matters is *your* mother, *your* father, *your* birth, *your* life, *your* death. Analyze and articulate *your* myths, *your* rituals, *your* conditioning, *your* patterns, the play *you're* acting out every day, the novel that is unfolding as *your* life. All I hope to do is to catalyze you to stop and think about your own story.

Personal writing is itself a way of shamanic healing. Journal writing, diaries, autobiography, even personal letters are ways of relating to yourself, discovering the truth about yourself and the people and realities of your life.

It feels good to keep a journal and fill it with yourself —poems, dreams, dialogues, portraits, letters, reminiscences, observations, reflections, insights, confessions, drawings, quotations. It means taking your life seriously, caring enough to see it honestly, to see and tell the truth. It should be a vital ongoing exercise in self-discovery: gradually finding your own voice, your own truths, your own story.

Get special notebooks and pens that you really like and reserve them for your personal writing.

A couple of easy ways to get started are through letters and reminiscences. Letter writing is becoming a lost art in this age of telephones and airplanes, so letters are an increasingly cherished and powerful way of communicating. And in a time when real intimacy with even our lovers, parents, and children is more and more difficult, letters allow us a ready way of overcoming our fear of expressing our feelings and the truth of our lives and thus are a route to truly intimate communications. So write letters not only to those who live at a distance, but to those you live with, sharing your feelings, experiences, memories, ideas.

You can also make a start on your life story by working with family photographs. Put together photos of yourself, your parents, siblings, friends, teachers, etc., from various stages in your life: baby pictures; pictures of parents, grandparents, etc.; school and college pictures; wedding pictures, and so on. Reflect on each and write down the special memories, feelings, and insights that the photos evoke.

Now here are some trailmarkers for your journey backward and forward as you discover your own life story. We will begin with the birth cycle, then move through childhood, puberty, and maturity to the final cycle—attending in each cycle to those sacred teachers and life tasks that need to be assimilated in order for us to move forward into enlightenment.

4. THE BIRTH CYCLE

The river she is flowing,
Flowing and growing;
The river she is flowing
Down to the sea.
Mother carry me,
A child I will always be.
Mother carry me,
A child I will always be.

traditional song

The birth cycle begins with conception and lasts for approximately five years. Mother is the sacred teacher of this cycle. She passes on her lessons through her body by example, guidance, attitude, energy, vibration. When a woman forgets her sacred function, it is destructive for herself, her child, her society, and her world.

Men with maternal instincts know how to nurture themselves and how to take care of their children. But it is mothers who pass the nurturing instinct on to their children. Body to body. It's that simple. The process begins in pregnancy, when the connection between the bodies and psyches is total. Here's where the baby gets the first experience of the presence or absence of a maternal instinct.

A mother's sacred role is to respect her baby's uniqueness and nurture its self-worth. She feeds her baby when it's hungry, not according to the schedule of some expert, and feeds the baby what it wants and not what is expected or routine. She allows her child to cry when hurt or sad, to sleep when tired. She thus acknowledges and reinforces the validity of the child's own internal messages. She teaches her child to trust itself.

In this way, she passes on her nurturing maternal instinct, aiding the child to know spontaneously how to answer the vital questions: "Who am I and what do I need?"

When a mother does her job of honoring her child's natural instincts, her child knows who it is and what it truly needs and wants without elaborate thinking and conscious effort. The child is becoming its own person, assured of its worth and its unique identity.

It's the mother's task to pass on this self-valuing, self-nurturing instinct to her child, not to "mother" the child for the rest of its life. In the birth cycle, you are meant to learn to become your own mother by integrating the maternal instinct. This sacred function takes about five years. If the mother performs her sacred task fully and well, then her job is fundamentally done. A mother who is effectively present for her child teaches her child to be attentive to, nurturing and affirming of, itself.

A mother can only give what she has received. She can only teach her child to care for itself as appropriately as she cares for herself. The more that women naturally value and nurture themselves, the better mothers they can be.

If a mother is physically or psychically absent during the child's initial five years, the child's struggle for a sense of self can be lifelong. Insufficiently mothered children grow up without an internalized maternal instinct: If they have been fed when they are not hungry or not fed when they are, put to bed when they feel wide awake or kept awake when they are sleepy, told they can't wear what they want to wear, molded (in many subtle ways) to conform to an image, schedule, or experience that is not their own, then they have been conditioned to distrust their own internal messages and end up too scared to be themselves, unable to know and take care of themselves properly. They are uncomfortable in their bodies, and have no strong sense of themselves and what they need. They identify with everyone else in a vain attempt to discover themselves, losing themselves in relationships, associations, possessions, roles—none of which fills the emptiness within. The radical insecurity resulting from their failure to actualize their nurturing instinct can be palpable and chronic.

With the depreciation of mothering in modern society, we're seeing the tragic results of generations of motherless children, or at least insufficiently mothered children. Millions of adults go around trying to tranquilize their pain and satisfy their insatiable hunger for security and approbation by sucking on cigarettes, losing themselves in alcohol, sex, drugs, work, and stuffing the perennial feeling of emptiness with food. More and more we are a nation of people who need some sort of fix, some sort of narcotized, altered state to get by. Some of us wouldn't be such ready junkies if we'd had the security of a mother's arms and the sweet ecstasy of her breast and a chance to develop and experience our unique way of being in the world.

The most prominent symptom of our collective lack of a maternal instinct is the polluting of our planet. Polluting the earth displays the same lack of mothering as polluting our bodies. There's little essential difference between filling ourselves with junk food and dumping noxious chemicals into the sea. Where is the mother?

It is little wonder that the original religions of the earth, up to the dawn of historic times, focused on the Mother Goddess. For it is mothering that gives us our essential well-being. The well-mothered child has a self-possession, bodily confidence, a boldness that seems just right, and I find that adults with such qualities inevitably were babies who were specially cherished by their mothers.

Mothers don't have to be the sole care givers to their young children. A lot of mothering can be done as well by fathers, grandmothers, grandfathers, and other care givers, but ideally the mother should be there regularly, fully giving the intimate mothering only she can give. And if she does it well, her primary job is done when the child is five or so. Mothering doesn't have to go on for decades to the detriment of the woman and the child.

If, like so many, your mothering was incomplete and your nurturing instinct is underdeveloped, it is time to begin the task of creative healing. Our mother lack is a wound that happens by degrees: some are totally deprived and others are only slightly hurt. But for all, the healing process involves becoming your own mother—really caring for yourself, recognizing and filling your own needs. Start with the basics, giving yourself just what you need to eat, giving yourself the time to sleep, to be alone, wearing just what you want to.

One special thing you can do is, for once, have a love affair with yourself. Treat yourself as you would treat a lover with whom you're passionately in love. Buy yourself flowers, make yourself delicious meals. Write to yourself about what makes you special, praising your special way of being, your accomplishments. Cherish time with yourself, luxuriating in your own company, doing just what you'd love to do. Take that trip, buy that car, rent that place you've always dreamed of.

People with the mother wound often have difficulty being alone. They always need to be with someone else to feel they truly exist, and thus end up in all sorts of destructively dependent relationships—with lovers, friends, coworkers, etc. You can begin to counter this black-hole syndrome by giving yourself the things you need and want—a nap, a fling, a day off, a little peace and quiet.

What wasn't learned instinctively now has to be consciously acquired. But the ultimate aim should not be, as it often seems to be in antiaddiction programs, to remain permanently in recovery, coping with a permanent wound. Rather we should aim at healing the wound and becoming fully free to be our true selves. Take, for instance, the issue of our relation to food and weight. If you eat only when you're truly hungry, and not for any other reasons (anger, sadness, consolation, boredom, etc.), and give yourself exactly what you want at a particular time (whether it's brussels sprouts or chocolates) and stop when your hunger is satisfied, you'll stay at your natural body weight. The body knows what it wants and needs, and once the emotional noise is shut off, you can get in tune with its naturally healthy ecology. Then you can apply this same philosophy to other areas of your life. Keep (or get) and wear just those clothes you really feel good in and get rid of the rest; so, too, with books, records, and other forms of entertainment. Most especially, begin to focus gradually on the vital components of your life—lover, family, friends, work—going after what you *really* want and need in every situation, every relationship. This is not base selfishness, but a nurturing self-fullness that allows you to be completely present for every person and every task in your life. If everyone traveled light, with just the real essentials, how much richer, freer, and direct all our relationships would be.

If it's instinctive for you to love and serve yourself, to appreciate and honor your being, thank your mother. If it's more or less difficult to do so, forgive her and heal yourself. For you know how hard it is to live with an insufficient nurturing instinct, and it must have been just as hard or harder for your mother. Our strengths and weaknesses are passed down, and it takes courage to break these downward cycles.

Even most of us who have made it to adulthood without self-destructing or becoming marginalized need to develop our nurturing instinct by treating ourselves with respect, honesty, kindness, caring, and attention. Listen for a while to the tapes automatically going on in your head day after day and you'll likely be surprised at how hard you are on yourself—how critical, disparaging, negating. All this negativity just leads wearily to more negativity, to self-fulfilling prophecies of disappointment. Pay attention over several days to what you do for yourself. You'll probably find that you spend loads of time responding to the needs and agendas of other people and very little time on your true wants and needs. One vital way to start talking to ourselves in a more affirming, empowering voice is through writing as a process of personal discovery that exorcises past devils and creates a rich present.

Here are some writing exercises that will get you underway:

1. Start your life story. Begin with your conception. What have you been told, what can you find out about the circumstances in which you came into being? Were your parents deeply in love? Were they young, older, happy, stressed, scared? Were they strangers—actual or virtual? Were you the fruit of an unconscious moment of passion, ignorance, or even hostility, or a cherished surprise, or a longed for and "planned" event? How did the seed and egg that made you come together? You could use charcoals, crayons, pencils, pastels to visualize your conception in a form, and make that drawing the first page of your life journal.

2. Then think about the time you spent in your mother's womb. What was it like to be in her body? Was she relaxed, happy, scared, uptight, resentful? How did she feel about her pregnancy? What were the circumstances of her life at the time? Was she working outside the home, taking care of your siblings or other kids, under stress of any kind, happy in her relationship with your father or unhappy? Was she alone? Write about this from your mother's perspective and then from your own. Then go on to your own birth. Were you born in a hospital, delivered vaginally or by caesarean, were there complications, how hard was it for your mother, was she alone except for nurses and doctor, and so on? And then describe your first months, your years until school. Interview your parents, brothers and sisters, aunts and uncles. Go through photo albums, home movies, etc.; it's amazing how full a picture you can come up with, and thereby know the truth of your early years. Some people, of course, use hypnosis, psychoanalysis, etc., to

recover babyhood/early childhood memories, especially painful, repressed events. I just ask myself the question and let the writing flow.

3. Write a series of portraits of your mother at different times in her life and from various points of view. Portray how she was when she was young, when you were born, when you were in school, when you left home, at your wedding, and now. Write from your point of view, from your father's, from that of an independent biographer. Even try to see her from the perspective of the universe, as the universal mother—the quintessence, the embodiment, of Mother.

4. Read these portraits aloud and watch for the assumptions, the beliefs, the judgments that underlie them. Tease out the unspoken framework of your perceptions and examine its elements with courage and care. What is true, what is false, what attitude do you want to adopt here and now?

5. Write a series of dialogues with your mother on every subject that is dear to you. What would you say or ask? What would she ask, respond? Just keep writing till there's nothing left to say.

Another rich avenue of discovery in freeing the mind is meditation. You can gain insight into your relationship with your mother and enhance the nurturing mother bond through contemplating her in various ways.

Mother meditation: Imagine your mother sitting across from you. Bring her into focus, get a feeling for her overall being—who she is, how she operates with people, in the world. What does this mother "gestalt" say to you? What emotions are evoked? Think of three things you love about your mother. Three things you hate. Three hopes for her. Three fears. Explore how all these qualities and dynamics

are also parts of you, parts that you may refuse to acknowledge and "own."

Imagine some form of physical contact with your mother.
Rocking her in your arms, massaging her feet, placing the
palm of your hand on her belly. Find a way to effectively
imagine and feel this intimate connection.

Now let your mother go, placing her opposite you in
your imagination. Look into her eyes, and search deep within
yourself to find the power and the courage to thank her and
to forgive her absolutely. Thank her for creating your body,
for nursing and clothing and caring for it. Forgive her
wholeheartedly for her failings, her weaknesses, her shortcomings, her mistakes, and tell her how you, of all people,
truly understand the challenges she faced. Thank her for
your strengths and infirmities, your blessings and curses,
your achievements and wounds, acknowledging that—like
a tree or an animal—you are perfect just as you are with
all your imperfections and that she is the source of your
being.

The first time I ever did a meditation like this was
during my Arica training. It affected me deeply. I felt my
mother's caring presence, her affectionate nature, her loyalty, as well as her self-doubt, her fear, her dependence. The
parts of her I refused to acknowledge were indelibly in-
grained in me. I remember being moved to tears as I imagined her in my arms like a baby, felt her warm breath
against my breasts. I held her so closely, so tightly, so ten-
derly, rocked her so sweetly that cleansing tears flowed for
both of us. She called me the next day, saying she had had
me intensely on her mind in the past day or so. I felt the
connection to her more than I ever had before, and our
relationship moved to a whole new level of mutual caring
and honesty.

Whatever your relationship to your mother (and therefore to your body), it's important to acknowledge the truth
of that relationship and its effect on you.

Many of us have had the experience of being mothered and of mothering that is our profoundest experience of grounded ecstasy—pure delight in being. I think of my son as he grows into adulthood. We are dividing, and yet we are still one. I keep in mind Erich Fromm's observation: "The mother-child relationship is paradoxical and, in a sense, tragic. It requires the most intense love on the mother's side, yet this very love must help the child grow away from the mother, and to become fully independent."[7] I can feel my son in me forever, a vital part of me that never goes away. Like dancers on a vast stage, no matter how far he is away, the bond, the interplay is always there, the invisible thread of love, the chemical choreography of blood in the vein. He is both my pupil and my teacher. For it is he who inducted me into the mysteries of mothering. I was surprised by my selfless, spontaneous loving and service, devotion and trust—a part of me I'd never have known otherwise. And it is I who taught him the joy and value of being who he is. He is my truest mirror, my honest reflection, my most profound joy, the subject of my deepest fears. My child connects me to the most primal part of myself. I well up with his tears, cringe with his pain, brighten with his smile, suffer with his disappointments. And if, as the Burmese proverb has it, "A motherless son is a fish in low water," I fondly hope I have opened him up to an ocean of possibilities to swim in.

I once wrote him this poem:

Meeting in
the rocking chair
day and night,
my breasts
full and bare
your tiny mouth
sucking me
into bliss

seducing me
past myself.
I fall behind
your eyes like wings
and we fly
you and I
to the outskirts of time
where angels sing
like Tibetan bells.
In grace.
In innocence.
In gratitude.
With you
I am finally me.

5. THE CHILDHOOD CYCLE

Whether you are wounded or blessed (or most likely some of both) in the first cycle of life, you then move into childhood and need to meet your father as your sacred teacher. He is mother turned inside out, the authority to her permission, the line through her circle, the worldly wise "no" to her cosmic "yes." Through your mother your self-image grows; through your father it becomes defined. In/out, wait for it/go for it, surrender/control, allow/demand, feminine/masculine. Between mother and father you learn to dance the tango of life.

Your mother taught you how to be in your body. Your father teaches you how to express your heart as he initiates you into the world of relationships with others. He teaches the art of how best to relate to another person, because he is the first person outside of yourself that you have to relate to, that is, build a relationship with.

You came out of your mother's body; that relationship is real and immediate. It is a psychic "given." You and your mother are inescapably one. Father is outside of you. He is your first friend and your task (and his teaching) is to connect to him. In the creation of this relationship, you build the foundation for all your future one-to-one relationships; you learn to relate to the world of people through your father. In your later life, you relate to people as your father related to you and you to him. It is from father that we either do or do not receive the ability to instinctively know the answer to the question, "What does this other person truly need from me?" It is from father that we first learn the art of give and take, of giving and receiving, the high commerce of friendship. It is the father's role to pass on the paternal instinct, the instinctive ability to relate appropriately to others, teaching loyalty, companionship, sharing, and fairness.

Your father teaches you to draw the line, to feel your own sense of authority, to balance your self-nurturing feeling of boundless permission. "The Child is father to the Man," as Wordsworth puts it. In this whole process you learn to become, to a greater or lesser degree, your own father, your own friend.

Your relationship to your father determines whether you can be yourself and express your heart, or whether you must achieve, perform, charm, seduce, compete, please, demand, negate or destroy to feel recognized. These patterns are created early. In all our one-to-one relationships we tend to do whatever we had to do to get daddy's attention and approval when we were a child. As Robert Frost put it, "You don't have to deserve your mother's love. You have to deserve your father's. He's more particular."[8]

All friends are fathers in disguise. If your father was there for you, giving you what you needed in the moment, responding from his heart to your heart, cheering you on and reining you in, affirming and consoling, cautioning and encouraging, then the world wears a welcoming face and you'll know how to be a friend. If he was present for you,

you will instinctively know how to be present for others. I remember watching my father taking care of his dying brother. My uncle had a brain tumor, and every day a new piece of his body didn't work. He got to the point where only his face moved, and there was my dad telling him stories, massaging his feet, lighting his damn cigarettes, giving him what he needed. I realized that this was the quality of attention I had become accustomed to.

To whatever degree your father didn't or doesn't know how to relate to you, he can't know how to relate to others. The distant, absent father is distant and absent in other relationships as well. He tends to relate on the surface and perform, hide his feelings, think and plan, judge and compare. He must analyze his relationships because they're not instinctive to him. He has to *decide* how and what to feel, making lists of people's good and bad qualities so he can determine whether to be in relationship to them. He doesn't dare to be spontaneous, because he can't trust himself to respond appropriately. So he develops pre-planned and market-tested ways of being with others. Fathers who are wounded are suffering. And they create children who are wounded.

People with a limited paternal instinct develop coping patterns. They become performers, flatterers, deliberators. They hide behind their work or their kids. They worry a lot about titles, credentials, status, wealth, prestige, about who's in and who's out, because they don't trust themselves to be able to respond to another person and be responded to just for who each is. They use money to win control, love, influence. They adopt some pose, some strategy that allows them to get by without really entering into relationships and commitments heart and soul, here and now. I know a kid whose father sent him elaborate presents on his birthday but never showed up himself. When he grew up he gave his dad all kinds of presents—a condominium in Florida, a baby grand piano, a trip to Paris—but he never showed up either. The person without an instinct for relating is, in any encounter with another person or in a social or collaborative situation, ill at ease, in pain, in deceit, and quietly desperate. It's no wonder they act so inappropriately so often.

Children with father wounds are everywhere—surely many of us. They're easy to spot. Without the heart in their day-to-day living, without the color of feelings, life is drab. They can go to all the right parties in all the right clothes and still never have a good time. Pervading their lives is a lack of élan, a theme of melancholy—regret, despair even— that underlies their apparently successful life stories. The spark is missing.

Since many more children now grow up without fathers or with part-time fathers only, whether because of divorce or because many men devote so much of their time to work and other activities rather than to fathering, the number of adult children of absentee fathers is astronomical and growing higher daily. Of course, single mothers and full-time mothers, as well as other parental figures, can and do supply some of the fathering role, and some women have strong paternal instincts to pass on. As we know, some fathers have strong maternal instincts and offer what mothers deficient in nurturing instincts can't offer. But prior to all our social arrangements and penchant for creating structures to fit our worldly goals, there is an elemental and natural power to men playing the paternal role and women playing the maternal role.

The ideal is to have a biological mother who teaches us how to be in a body and trust ourselves, and a biological father who teaches us how to express our hearts. Just having parents doesn't guarantee success. Natural parents can fail their natural children—and adoptive, single, or foster parents can raise their children with instincts intact, as can parents who themselves have been wounded but through awareness and devotion have made the quantum leap into conscious parenting. My dad was one of these.

I've worked a lot with people with father wounds. I had a physician study with me who related to everyone as doctor to patient. It was as if he couldn't take off his white coat even for his lovers. He's not alone. Think of the talk show host who can't talk to someone unless there's a microphone between them. Actors who never seem to leave the stage. Executives who run their families like they run their business. Trial lawyers who map out strategies for all their relationships as if they are going to trial. Awareness of this "act" is the beginning of healing this wound.

It seems almost everyone grew up without enough fathering. If mothering has been insufficiently valued in our society, what about fathering? Regarded as a minor sideline, the father's job has been reduced to treasurer and warden. A woman in one of my workshops wrote this poem that captures the experience of so many children:

> *Daddy lives*
> *behind a newspaper,*
> *smoking cigarettes;*
> *always reading,*
> *no voice,*
> *no words,*
> *no touch;*
> *just there, behind*
> *the paper wall.*

And here's a piece of theater dialogue I wrote for two friends; I call it "Father in Staccato":

My father is a lawyer.

                                   My father is a doctor.

I became a lawyer.

I became a doctor.

I lived in the same town.

I moved away.

My father didn't touch me.

I didn't touch my father.

My father didn't know me.

I didn't know my father.

My father really loved me.

I really loved my father.

My father was my hero.

My father was my heart.

I thought I was just like him.

I grew up to play his part.

In fact, I'm not just like him.

He never falls apart.

My father was together.

He was always in control.

Not together with me.

My father couldn't see me.

My father can't see now.

He couldn't look me in the eye.

Me, I think he's scared to look.

He was lost in a lie.

Broken dreams in his scene

That pretend will get you by.

He gave all he had.

My father wasn't bad.

He simply wasn't there.

No one taught him how to care.

And I really love him.

And he really loves me.

And I really love him.

And he really loves me.

And I really love him.

Happily, fathering seems to be making a comeback, but there remain the countless walking wounded who grew up without adequate paternal care by fathers who themselves lacked strong relational instincts.

This father wound, like the mother wound, has reached epidemic proportions. It is everywhere, breeding loneliness, alienation, distrust, deceit. We lie to each other about what we think and feel and do, and don't remember how to tell the truth. And we desperately need to speak and to hear the truth. We readily see right through others' efforts to hide their pain, shame, disregard. We forget that they also see right through us. They see the fear, anger, sorrow—the real energy we struggle to mask. We pretend to care about each other, but end up sharing the worst of ourselves, the stuff that doesn't work. We're as predictable as daily headlines, as spirited as Muzak.

Father wounds take a great toll on our intimate relationships. If we don't know how to talk to each other or to be together without talking, if we don't know how to give and receive, how can we make love? How can we move one another? How can we be touching? How can we be real? We all expect to have wonderful intimate relationships, but how can we be real lovers if we don't know how to be true friends?

Can you remember your last real heart-to-heart conversation, where you really hooked into each other, following every move, every gesture, every wave of emotion, riding the waves together, connected? When did you last partake of such holy communion?

Communion heals the father wound. Communion with friends, lovers, parents, strangers, even enemies. But mostly with friends. Through hard trial and error and working with thousands of people, I've discovered that the heart needs to open up as fully as possible. It is a waste of time to pretend that we can't be hurt. If we're going to be fully alive, we have to be ready to get hurt and even to hurt others. Otherwise, we're dead. Or immobilized in protective armor.

In vulnerability one practices the art of friendship, the art of the heart. It is an essential spiritual practice.

If you don't do it instinctively, you must do it consciously. Stop and focus on your relationships and let them each teach you what you need to know. The more you give to them, the more you will get back. The more attention you pay, the more natural relating will feel, until the impulse to take special care of your relationships becomes internalized and instinctive.

It's interesting to make a list of your friends, then sit and contemplate what each has to teach you. Meditate on each name and ask yourself, "What does this person really need from me?"; "What do I really need from him or her?" Keep asking until answers come.

Who nourishes you? How? Why? Who drains you? How? Why? Who do you avoid? How? Why? Who do you reach out to? How? Why?

Bring your relationships into the moment, including the one with your father. Erase the past, stay out of the future with all its expectations. Let yourself be surprised. Practice "loving the one you're with." Everyone you know is dying for some real attention, someone who really hears what they're saying, sees their vision, cheers them on into the heights and depths of being real.

We need relationships that are alive, vital, changing, moving—relationships that move through all the rhythms. Sometimes they flow, sometimes they pulse, sometimes they erupt, sometimes they lilt along, and sometimes they're very still. It is particularly important to have a moving relationship with one's father, as this relationship is the key to all other friendships.

Here are some exercises to help you discover and befriend your father. With courage and creative reflection often we can forge anew a very special bond of friendship, regardless of time or distance. Or we can at least learn concretely the truth of our childhood and determine what aspects of fathering we need in order to complete our childhood cycle.

1. An easy way to begin learning about our childhood cycle is with the mirror opposite of the father/child relationship you may have missed out on. Make friends with a young child, age five, six, or seven. Children at this age are usually spontaneous, warm, enthusiastic, and they don't put up with bullshit. They live here and now. They will be emotionally direct, demand flexibility and patience, and reward your attention with a joy in being that can't be measured.

2. Write down your memories of your father before you were five, and what you've been told about him. What was he like? Where was he? Recall his varied guises, smells, habits; the way he talked, sang, cried (or didn't).

3. Sit back, relax, and feel yourself moving backwards in time like a movie in reverse. Stop when you get to five years old. Imagine your five-year-old self in a familiar room with your father. How do you feel? Do you make contact? What kind? Are you touching, talking, laughing, cowering, uncomfortable, insecure? Fast forward to about ten years old and see yourself in the same room: how do you relate to your father; how does he relate to you?

4. Write a dialogue between your father and yourself at age ten. If you can't, that will tell you something.

5. Who is he? Capture him in an image, a metaphor, a quintessential photo, a characteristic statement, a telling story.

6. In your journal, visualize your relationship to your father in an "energy drawing" that clearly conveys the undercurrent as well as the surface waves that flow between you and your father.

7. Write a capsule account of your father's life story, tracing the movement of his life from infancy through childhood and adolescence to adulthood, middle age, and final years. Did he or is he likely to die satisfied, fulfilled, serene?

8. How would your mother tell his story? How would he?

9. How would you speak to your father if you were his friend, not his child? What would you say as his best friend? Somebody has to break the wall of silence: pick up the phone; get on the plane; talk real things out heart to heart. He's probably as lonely as you are. Are you afraid of your father? Afraid for him? Are you angry with him? How does he bring you joy? What's the most compassionate thing you could do for him? Let it all out now. The healing will be wonderful for you both.

10. Since your father was your first friend, you probably treat your friends the way he treated you. Write portraits of three different friends, and your relationship to each. Read them over and over, looking for repetitive patterns, positive as well as negative. Do you run each relationship or do you get pushed around? Do you play hard to get? Are you flirtatious, overbearing, timid? How do you relate? Do you relate at all, or do you perform, plan, seduce, etc.?

Maybe it's instinctive for you to move heart to heart and easy for you to know what another needs; maybe you come from your heart most of the time. If so, you have your father to thank. If not, forgive him: this is also his pain. You do have something in common.

Life is raw material that cries out to be transformed into art—survival art rooted in truth, carved into poems, into songs, into albums, into communications straight from the heart. You can turn your relationship to your father into art. Think about it, write about it, embrace your childhood, your heart.

Meditating on your father can also be rewarding: Sit back, take a deep breath, settle into a comfortable position.

Father meditation: Imagine your father sitting opposite you: how does he hold himself, how does he look, what is the basic impression he makes on you—weariness, anger, impatience, ebullience, calm?

Think of three things you love about him, three qualities you find endearing. Think of three things that put you off, alienate you. Reflect on how all these qualities are in you as well, on how much alike you are, how intimately connected.

Look your dad in the eye. Let your feelings about him surface, and imagine saying them to him. Empty your heart of all the things you might have choked back for years, telling him everything you feel till there's nothing left. Imagine what he would say in response and let him say his piece. Then breathe calm into the empty space that is left.

Imagine, too, making physical contact with your father, touching him, holding his hand, hugging him, rocking him. Let the blocked affection for him flow and receive his in return.

Then let him go back to his place. Look him in the eye again and search your heart for the courage to thank and forgive him, to forgive and thank yourself. Forgive him for his weaknesses and failings; thank him for making you who you are and being there for you when he was.

When I have meditated on my dad, I've appreciated his generosity, his loyalty, his serenity. I've acknowledged his stubborn pride, his prejudices, his timidity—all part of me. I've swooped him up in my arms, held him close and rocked him like a baby, wiped the tears from his face and pressed his ear to my heart.

Everyone has a father. Some active and reporting for duty, some missing in action. Some out of step with the beat of their own hearts. Some too busy to relate to the most important charges in their lives. If we haven't found our father outside, we have to find him within, and to reconnect with our father if and when we can. It's a sacred task, a vital undertaking.

As we heal ourselves, we release our parents in some beautiful way to heal themselves. I've seen this pattern repeat itself in many lives. It has inspired and given me hope. We can effect change by changing. And what a gift to be able to heal your parents just by healing yourself. We have the power to give them back the freedom to be who they really are—wounded, human, vulnerable, not giants in a fairytale or society's police force. But real people— your people.

As we become our own parents, become whole, it lifts a psychic burden off our parents' shoulders; they no longer need worry about what they did and didn't do for you, and are free to become themselves.

6. THE PUBERTY CYCLE

Most of us associate puberty with our early teenage years. But this sorting-out cycle can last from the upheaval of early adolescence to the determined searching of our late twenties.

Human beings simply don't fall mature from the nest. It takes a lot of time and work to develop into adults. And to find our center, we have to explore our outer edges. Our being doesn't come readily programmed by nature; we have to discover and take responsibility for who we uniquely are in relation to ourselves, others, and society.

Puberty is the time for the psychic seeds planted in the birth and childhood cycles to blossom. Time for us to become our own source of permission and authority, to dream our own dreams, follow our own visions, work out our own steps on the dancing path. Here's where we catalyze our internal instinct, our own sense of distinct inner direction, what we're all about. It's a chaotic period for the psyche: we shatter bonds to all authority outside ourselves and learn to change in a flash—up, down, in, out—but all in line with our inner drive. Puberty is our declaration of independence.

With the growth of the internal instinct, we learn to walk the edge between all the lines. We improvise the dance of control/surrender, leader/follower, masculine/feminine, open/closed. We're faced with infinite opportunities, choices, dilemmas, the underlying dynamics of which are risk and experimentation. Only by pushing off from shore, leaving behind the apparent safety of the known, can we set our own course. We end up tossed on uncharted waters. And we sail mostly in the dark. We have to test, to probe, to explore, to push.

What are my limits? What do I like? What do I do and how am I supposed to do it? Only by venturing into the unknown do the answers come. Thus, we need space to take chances and fail, to be responsible for our decisions and their consequences. Only with such personal freedom can we learn to trust ourselves, to take responsibility for the quality of our lives.

But because mothering and fathering tend to be so diffuse and erratic in our culture, we often arrive at puberty without the strong nurturing and relational instincts that allow us to step out boldly and assuredly on the path of individual self-discovery. And parents usually compensate and have to play catch-up for not concentrating more on mothering and fathering in the first ten years. They rely on teachers, teen peers, counselors, group leaders, or even the police to impose what has failed to be internalized—a sense of self and a sense of others.

The sad, unruly result is that just when we need lots of room to work out our own moves, our parents and various societal institutions begin to hem us in with rules and schedules, achievement goals and punishments for failure. And precisely because we are indeed handicapped in taking care of ourselves and effectively relating to others, all the strictures and hoop-jumping seem necessary for our own good and that of society.

The whole drive toward individuation is fueled by the sexual energy that has been building since our birth and now suddenly electrifies all our feeling and thinking. At our most primal level we are sexual beings. Sexual energy fuels our life drive and forges our deepest connections to ourselves and others. We were born to be turned on, set aglow with the flow of primal life energy, enlivened and made whole by the cellular dance of orgasm. We were born in bodies to experience the fullness of sexual energy— alone and in relationship, in our youth and old age, in its masculine and feminine modes, on its surface and to its depths.

Much of our social conditioning and many institutions are antisensual and antisexual: it's believed that sensuality and sexual energy too easily disrupt, even undermine plans, empire-building, and important agendas. Traditional organized religions have declared war on sex. Most governments discourage its full expression. Schools are reluctant to teach it. To all those interested in maintaining control, sex is the enemy. Just think how disruptive puberty is in the current context of controls and expectations. But it doesn't have to be. In other cultures, e.g., traditional African and Native American tribes, the onset of puberty is celebrated and accommodated. There are dancing and singing rituals that enhance young people's bodily expressiveness and emotional range; the initiation into sexual expression is gradual and guiltless. There really would be a lot less precipitous and problematic teenage sex if kids were given ample opportunity and guidance in exploring the full range of their sensuality in nonsexual ways. I'd love it if all children were taught to do yoga, aikido, massage, African dancing, and Middle Eastern dancing as wonderful ways to be fully in their bodies as sensual beings. But induction into sensuality is not valued by our still puritanical and intellectually oriented culture, and we usually learn to be at home in our sexual bodies later in life, if at all.

Still, youth is about more than sex. It is about becoming our own person, including, of course, our own sexual self. Physically we are a unique fusion of our mother and father, and psychically we need to blend the maternal and paternal instinct of our earlier cycles into an individuating instinct that grounds us in our distinctive perspective, style, energy. We need to find our own way of dressing, moving, speaking, acting. The easy solution in the search for style is just to adopt what's around, to yield to peer pressure; but the real point of admiring Madonna, say, was not to dress and be like her but to follow her daring in creating her own distinctive style. We need to search for a path with heart, a way of being and working that fits us uniquely. For example, to focus on a career not merely to get by, or to satisfy someone else's expectations and agenda, but because it's what we love to do.

Searching and experimenting requires room from parents (who ideally have done their jobs and can now back off), and requires cooperation from school and society. It's been suggested that really intense teaching of languages, mathematics, etc., should occur in our early years, from ages two or three to eleven or twelve, when we are wide open to the play of learning, and that the teenage years should allow for much more unstructured explorations in art, music, dance, travel, writing, etc., all with the aim of allowing our distinctive independent spirit to flower. It is during these years that our internal instinct is born.

People who don't learn to think, feel, or act for themselves lack the spontaneous ability to be their true natural selves in all the situations of life. They're always imitating, operating out of fear or coercion, living someone else's dream or agenda. For in adolescence you should be your own sacred teacher, and the playing out of your hunches, the experimenting with styles and paths, is integral to becoming your own person for life. Parents and others need to risk and honor their children's growing independence, channeling and inviting it in fruitful directions.

If we failed to develop our internal instinct, genuine independence in the puberty cycle, we now need to nurture it. Our internal instinct lets us know what's going on, and how to relate to various situations. Without the internal instinct, we never know quite what to do; our life is full of hesitation and dependence on outside determinants. The remedy for this is to do now what needed to be done in adolescence: risk experimenting, discover what you really want and go for it, even though it may be against all conventional wisdom. Dare to change things, start new things, change jobs, travel. Practice saying yes and no definitively, consciously, independently, even if your head is still full of doubts and fears. Develop your capacity for critical thinking, taking nothing for granted, questioning everything. For the security of dependence is actually the insecurity of not controlling your own life, or being your own person. In puberty we unleash the power of our mind—to establish modes of thought and action that will serve us all our lives.

The power of your mind can heal any psychic wounds. Use it to confront your conditioning; if you missed any part of the puberty cycle, now is the time to complete it. The ideal is an inner marriage of the maternal and paternal, the male and female, which blends the wisdom to know who you are and what you need with the strength to stand up for yourself and relate to others' real needs. It's a delicate balancing act, a free form dance in which you're challenged to create your own steps. Find your own voice; take control of your own story. Otherwise, you sing secondhand songs, become part of someone else's plot.

Here are some exercises to stimulate the completion of the adolescent cycle:

1. Write your mom a letter from your heart. Share any fear, anger, or sadness you feel in relationship to her. Any joy. Any feeling of compassion. Say what you couldn't say when you were a teenager. Use each of these expressed emotions as a jumping off point into the stream of your own consciousness. What do *you* have to say, how do *you* want to say it? Find your own style. Say everything. Hold nothing back. No censorship. No control. Let images, memories, reflections, dreams, wounds, blessings pour onto the page.

2. Write a letter to your father straight from your heart. Start with the fears in your relationship to him, move to anger, then sadness, joy, compassion. Get in touch with these feelings and the attitudes they create. Let them all go on paper. Don't stop till you're empty.

3. When you have nothing left but compassion for your parents, you are clean. Burn the letters, if you want, and scatter their ashes in the wind.

    (For me, recognizing my parents was an awesome task. I thought my parents were perfect and that I was worthless. Writing these letters, I was able to sort out my feelings, put flesh on their bones, express all kinds of unexpressed emotions in relation to them. I was able to see how I was wounded but also to see especially how much I'd been blessed. In recognizing their sacred roles in my life, and their courageous efforts to fulfill them, my whole perspective on life lightened and freshened.)

4. Write a self-portrait, an autobiography in your own style. Organize the story around the life cycles and sacred teachers.

5. Sketch your own sexual history. Pay attention to all the

details, all the people. Make a list of your lovers, all of them. Study it. What does it tell you? About your body? Your heart? Your mind? Your sexual development? Imagine all of them in the same room. With just you.

6. Describe in detail the feminine aspects of yourself, the nurturing, receptive, night-moon side of yourself. Name her. Embrace her.

7. Describe the masculine sides of yourself, the analytical, outgoing, aggressive, daytime side. Name him. Embrace him.

8. Imagine and write out a love affair between him and her, how they complement, mesh, conflict, inspire. Let the affair blossom into a marriage, a lifelong commitment.

9. Write a portrait of three friends from the aspect of the interplay between their female and male sides. See how they are mother/father, sister/brother, daughter/son, and delight in the discovery.

You can also practice a simple meditation on yourself. Close your eyes and imagine yourself seated on a pillow across from you. Look honestly, compassionately, at the overall image you project, the shape of your consciousness. What does it tell you about yourself? Where are you holding tension? How deep does your breath flow? If you were an animal, what animal would you be? If you were a place in nature, a color, a musical instrument, a body of water, a sound, a taste, a precious stone, what would you be?

Think of both your inner and outer life. What is going on inside you—your dreams, fantasies, concerns, feelings? Are there memories that haunt you? Do your attitudes trap or inspire you? What are your deepest desires? What's happening on the outside? Does your outer reality match your inner reality? How are you expressing yourself in the world? Do you act and speak your inner truth? Or have you created a division between who you really are and how you present yourself? Ask yourself: "What are my gifts? What was I born to do? Am I doing it? If not, why?" Wait for answers. Don't accept any excuses. Remember that all the questions and all the answers vital to life are within you.

7. THE SUPREME CHALLENGE: THE CYCLE OF MATURITY

The transition to the cycle of maturity should take place by age thirty in our culture. But the transition often never is completed: we remain, in many aspects of our lives, infants, children, adolescents. In the cycle of maturity we face the supreme challenge of what Freud identified as the essential human task: finding love and work. But we arrive at the stage of giving ourselves to a committed lifelong relationship and to our vocation often without having resolved the challenges of the earlier stages. So marriage ends up being more therapy rather than a mature relationship; work becomes more a matter of making a living, than an encompassing solution to the challenge of making a difference, a contribution.

In my work I've run into lots of people searching for enlightenment. Many imagine that it involves following some hot new guru or getting into some group or esoteric practice. Maybe. But having a family is another way. The challenge of being in a loving, committed relationship for life and of raising children poses all the essential challenges needed to bring out the best in you. Committing yourself to work that is meaningful to you is another path to enlightenment. These paths to wisdom, which include marriage and family, work, a spiritual group, are maps for enlightenment that may be followed either separately or collectively.

In the late sixties and early seventies, my whole culture seemed to be fixated in puberty, and I was definitely part of my culture. I and everyone around me were fleeing from responsibility and society as fast as we could. Since adulthood seemed an unrewarding mess of boredom and violence, we decided to just avoid it altogether and retreat back from its edges to the earlier stages of life. And then a lot of people over thirty who had repressed the challenges of puberty in their rush to maturity now freaked out and joined the rush back to adolescence. The flight from responsibility is still a large part of our culture, since maturity is so much identified with dull, jingoistic, bourgeois living.

But there's a lot more to maturity than a three-car garage, a fistful of credit cards, the right kind of spouse, and the appropriate number of kids. As puberty is the time to find out what you have to give, maturity is the time to give it. It's the time to make your distinctive contribution. Society, in the widening concentric circles of family, local community, country, world, is the sacred teacher of the maturity cycle. In maturity we're called to live in permanent and responsible relationship to others: life partner, children, parents, extended family, friends and associates, and the wider society. Maturity involves knowing and taking responsibility for one's part in the interrelated and interdependent facets of our life in the world.

This fraternal instinct, this sense of community, finds expression in our physical, emotional, and intellectual interaction with others. The sacred task in this cycle is to serve society and at the same time serve ourselves. Authentic adult living requires constant creative interplay between our common cause with others and our own special needs and gifts. The challenge is to give to others what you uniquely have to give, while still retaining your individuality and taking care of your own needs.

The dialectic between individual and group is resolved differently in different societies. Compare individual rights and social arrangements in Russia vs. the United States vs. India vs. China vs. Sweden vs. Switzerland vs. Israel! Society in its conventions, structures, and rules, can, like the other sacred teachers, wound as well as educate, sabotage as well as support your journey along the dancing path.

If society has a soul—if its maternal, paternal, and internal instincts are embodied in its shared meanings, values, structures—then it can support the mature balance between individuality and social responsibility. Its easiest to see such balance in small traditional societies, such as mountain villages in Crete or Pygmy tribes in Africa.

If society is fragmented, soulless inside and out—a collection of individuals regenerating the vicious cycle of parents wounding children who grow up to wound their children, however unwittingly—then achieving maturity becomes a heroic task. It requires remarkable individual effort and insight, special help, and incorporation into at least small islands of social sanity in the midst of the insanity of the wider world. In a soulless society, the need for people to attain maturity in love and work becomes even more vital. For only healthy individuals can heal a soulless society.

Maturity involves the synthesis of all you've learned. It's the time of the soul, the essence of all you are. As adolescence unleashed the mind, childhood the heart, and the birth cycle the body, maturity brings out the soul. The keys to maturity are commitment and responsibility. You put behind the experimentation and provisionality of adolescence and commit yourself to someone, to something. It's time to stop studying, stop preparing, stop searching and to start teaching, doing, manifesting, producing. It's no longer spring training; it's time to play for keeps. The rehearsals are over, the show is on.

Maturity demands the equanimity and self-confidence to be fully engaged yet sufficiently detached to assess what's going on. To be both actor and witness, no longer locked into the roller coaster of life's ups and downs and shifting attachments, but now taking responsibility that things turn out as you want them to.

Thus in our sexual development, maturity is the age of commitment, of truly going all the way. It is the age of intimacy. Sexual energy, instead of being diffused, is focused on one person, a life mate, a soulmate. If we're ready, i.e., if we've completed the prior cycles, we can now drop our masks and poses and enter into a relationship of full trust and loyalty. Our soulmate is our friend and lover, student and teacher, our day-to-day partner who dances us deeper into our essence. Our soulmate is our mirror and our vital trading partner in the exchange of life energies. Intimacy moves soul to soul. Its total surrender bares the soul. For our ego can't be intimate; it must always control things. True intimacy cuts through all the layers of our ego as each partner completes him- or herself through the other.

In maturity, we cannot truly experience sexual intimacy or live up to the demands of committed love without the preparation of the preceding cycles. Inexperience and ignorance, repression and resentment, whether in body, heart, or mind, undermine so many relationships, even those that are long-lived. Any gaps in our development can profoundly affect our primary relationships, no matter how strong they are. In a committed relationship, we can no longer hide by changing partners; our strengths and weaknesses soon come out.

More often than imagined, sexual immaturity and repression can sentence people to living desperately alone. Inexperienced and scared, they end up isolated and lonely, able to create only a bad or superficial relationship, investing their sexual energy in their work, suppressing it with alcohol and drugs, or denying it in the name of some divine calling.

On the other hand, repressed earlier cycles can sweep into the seeming tranquility of mature life with the force of a tornado. For example, the need for friendship denied in the childhood cycle erupts into homosexual or hetero-sexual affairs with people who hold the promise of being totally understanding best friends. Or an unfulfilled ado-lescence can shatter family, career, and social standing by erupting into midlife promiscuity. Belated puberty breeds the Playboy ideal, topless bars, "open" marriages, divorce courts, and children competing with their parents to dis-cover their sexual identity.

Whereas in the course of natural and complete devel-opment, commitment and intimacy are not an imposition from outside but an evolution from within.

The challenge of meaningful work, work with soul and spirit, is an equally vital task of the maturity cycle. We need to fulfill our potential and make our contribution. But the incompletion of earlier cycles tends to leave us without the solid confidence, relational skills, and inde-pendence necessary to forge a meaningful and satisfying career. Rather, jobs become one of the primary areas in which people perpetuate their insecurity, alienation, and dependence.

As with love, finding the right work requires courage, commitment, and a healed past. It takes care, candor, and insight to discover our own true interests and talents. Often we know in our heart of hearts just what it is we're good at and love to do, and others can help us identify it as well. The key is to free ourselves of others' expectations, or our own indoctrination. We need the courage to change course, to risk traveling the path with heart. Gauguin packed in his bank clerk's job and headed for the South Pacific; we can at least risk changing jobs.

Once you discern the path, commitment is what makes a vocation a reality. Quickly survey a dozen successful, creative people whom you admire and I'm sure you'll find that the essential ingredient in their achievements is an extraordinary dedication to what they do. They don't make excuses for their weaknesses or dwell on disadvantages;

they just get the job done with a special degree of seriousness. They take their lives and their work seriously. And the miracle is that when that happens, the work seems less like a burden or obligation and more like play, more like fun.

The other crucial element in reaching maturity lies in healing the past. And the cycle of maturity is the age in which we must get on with the business of healing the wounds of infancy, childhood, adolescence.

Here are some exercises to bring home the points raised in this section:

1. Write a detailed account of your primary intimate relationships up to now. What was good about them? What was not? What about the sexual dimension of these relationships? Did it change or remain the same? Were there common patterns?

2. Do a portrait of the ideal intimate relationship you would like to have. What would be its essential elements? What would you have to do to make it happen?

3. Are you doing the right work? Is it interesting, fulfilling, challenging, fitting? Go over your work history from your childhood and adolescent fantasies and expectations, through college and/or other career preparation and through your various jobs. What are the patterns? The unfulfilled dreams?

4. Do a sketch of what you ideally would like to be doing for a living in order to exploit your talents and concerns. What are the key elements? How could you make it happen?

5. Write about how your life and work fit into society. What contributions are you making? Are you making a difference for the better, the worse, or not at all? What might you be able to do?

8. THE FINAL CYCLE

I'm still in the midst of the maturity cycle, not yet in the final cycle. But death has been a part of my experience in every cycle, and the tranquility, solitude, peace, universality, and centeredness that are the promise of the last cycle already beckon me. I can readily understand all those thousands of people choosing early retirement these days if retirement means not cessation of work, but retiring into what matters most—entering into the richest, fullest phase of life.

The last cycle begins at around sixty, presaged by menopause (male as well as female), and ends when your body gives out. In this last teaching on the path we confront our mortality, the central human truth that we are born to die. We receive this final teaching from life itself—the universe, as sacred teacher, is the final stage of enlightenment. Not blissed-out enlightenment, but everyday, here-and-now enlightenment: wisdom about living, being here/now. The final destination is to live in zero gravity, in the moment, no past, no future. Living without attachments—to people, places, possessions, philosophies, to life, to living. Letting go. Letting be. Just being. Only being. And that is everything.

Death is the ultimate letting go from the material plane of reality. Enlightenment is the ultimate letting go on the psychic plane of reality. Death releases us from life. Enlightenment releases us within it.

To arrive at the last cycle of life having fulfilled the tasks of earlier cycles is to be naturally prepared for enlightenment. We are all born to grow wise with age. Older people, if they can put the past healingly behind them, have within them the wisdom of life. In the last phase, having completed the tasks of individuality, we are free to become universal citizens, seeing our connection to everyone and everything, contemplating the universal truths. It is in forging our connection to all that we develop our instinct for the eternal, the spirit in us that transcends all the things of life, including our own individuality.

How important it is to enter the last phase of life with innocence, experienced but uncorrupted, unjaded. Open to the final adventure, the way we came in. That's why it made so much sense for traditional societies to have older people and children share so much of their life together, blending the wisdom and focused caring of age with the fresh innocence and openness of childhood. Both are on the edge of eternity, close to the source.

Tragically, the elderly in our society are mostly marginalized and made to feel unwanted and useless. For them seniority is cruel and the death cycle dark and terrifying, when instead it should be a joyous path to the light.

The final cycle is a time to surrender the reins of control and ambition. It's time freed for following impulses of being, feeling, thinking. It's freedom from convention, freedom from concern for what's nice, convenient, or ingratiating.

Ideally, one increasingly enters into a still center. From the flowing energy of infancy, through the staccato pace of childhood and the chaos of adolescence, beyond the lyrical rhythm of maturity, we move into the dynamic stillness of living in the spirit.

In the last cycle, in which death becomes part of life, and not its end, the thrust of our sexual energy gradually turns inward. It is not that older people give up sex, for it is known that older people can and do have rich sexual lives. The last cycle can be a time to complete the earlier sexual cycles. Still, the direction of our energy shifts. It takes more of our energy resources to accomplish the basic tasks of life, and we gradually need to spend more time and energy taking care of and loving ourselves. Too, if we are fortunate enough to live out our days with our life lover, we will dwell more in the afterglow and stillness of lovemaking than in its pursuit, and our caring will acquire a thousand other forms of basic expression. Ideally we will experience a shift toward fulfilled celibacy, the marriage of the male and female energies within us. Vibrant celibacy in old age is a celebration of wholeness, not a denial of sexuality, as we advance to a deep inner sensuality, a love affair with life, a tantric union with all living things. We are not abstaining, but containing. There's a natural loss of interest in genital sexuality, and our sexual energy spreads out into the whole of our life—holding hands, being together, eating, sleeping, walking together. At the end of life, our sexuality comes full circle and, as with children, is drawn into our daily life, our very existing.

If we arrive at the last cycle without having achieved the intimacy of maturity, our last years may be spent in pain, loneliness, and confusion. But if we do achieve intimacy, even if our life partner dies before we do, we have the deep satisfaction in body, heart, and mind that we lived fully to anchor our inward turning. But how many people divorce out of failure and frustration in middle age and spend their last years beset by needs that friends and children can't fulfill?

Similarly, many enter the last stage of life feeling worthless and bereft because they no longer have the identity with their work or their job and the feeling of being needed. But if one finds a path of work, of right livelihood that is *more* than just a paycheck, a status provider, or a way to spend one's time, such vocations tend to grow and change naturally with age and there will always be the enduring satisfaction of having made a distinctive contribution, and of having developed one's talents.

If we arrive at the final cycle without healing many of our psychic wounds, old age offers none of the peace and contemplation it's meant to. Whatever neurotic patterns you may have developed over the years become chiseled in stone, a prison that traps your spirit in a body that hasn't the resiliency to move through the healing rhythms, a heart whose emotional arteries are clogged, and a mind closed to movement or change.

How sad are those who go toward death "kicking and screaming," vituperative and seeking still more retribution, denying the truth of their lives to the bitter end. It doesn't have to be that way.

The eternal instinct propels us toward death consciously, with eyes open, accounts balanced. How wonderfully inspiring are older people blossoming into their quintessential selves, imbued with humor and compassion as they view the passing tragicomedy of personal and global politics.

A few years ago I had my own close encounter with death. I spent six months with my dying father, trying to choreograph his dance toward death. When it turned out that he had terminal lung cancer and only months to live, he looked to me to walk him to death just as he walked me into life. He wanted me to decipher the mysteries, to decode the master plan, and I felt so fragile and inadequate. All I had to give him was my attention and my love and the bits of knowledge I'd accumulated along the way. Here was the real test of the worth of all I'd learned. What do you have to give to your dying father?

It was fitting that the sacred teacher of my childhood, of my heart, my first friend, in his dying led me into new and deeper levels of shamanic healing. His death was also my rebirth.

Dying is usually a process that is as active as it is passive. It is as much a doing as an undergoing. It involves active choices and attitudes as well as letting go. It's a final dance with elaborate steps, and we usually have to improvise. Of course, some people die in a flash without ever knowing what hit them, but others like my dad prepare for death, aware of it as a process.

In six months, he reciprocated my mother's unwavering devotion by teaching her in a dozen ways what she needed to know to carry on alone. It was time to say goodbye to those dear to him. Time to say thank you. A bittersweet time.

I gave him everything I could: tools to heal his psyche, to knit his fragmented self together for the final journey into eternity, to foster the union of his body, heart, mind, soul, and spirit. I strove to have us acknowledge dying as a deeply religious experience, a door to enlightenment, to being whole and at peace.

All healing journeys begin and end in the body. To mitigate the cancer eating him up, he chose to nourish his body with raw foods. To complement this health food regime, I began doing all sorts of relaxation meditations with him. His terror of death had locked his body in tension. I'd sit beside him and begin in a slow, deep, relaxed voice to calm him down, to call his spirit into his body.

I'd light candles and incense to heighten the sacred character of this last rite of passage. Often I'd play soft, relaxing music, sometimes with a friend or two accompanying me on flute, drums, or synthesizer. Healing is an art. And I would respond to the energy of the day or hour, sometimes drifting into a meditative trance in which I would take him with me deep into his body, and the words would come: "Feel your body sink into the bed, heavy and relaxed. Imagine a warm wave of energy softly swirling around your feet and entering into your toes, relaxing all the tiny little muscles and tendons. Your feet feel warm and heavy as they sink toward the bed, and this energy moves into your ankles, massaging them, releasing all the tension in your feet. You feel your calves open to receive this warm, healing energy, golden rays of oceanside sun. . . ." And so on through his whole body.

I massaged him two or three times a day to keep him relaxed and in direct touch with my caring. And I made sure he walked every day in the fresh air. I had to keep him moving. Moving arouses energy, confidence, a sense of worth and vital being; sedentariness yields passivity, timidity, a sense of uselessness and powerlessness. Just watch the difference between older people who walk and exercise energetically and those who don't; the energetic are healthier not only physically but in every other way.

Dealing with my father's emotions was more difficult. He had feelings within him buried since childhood: hidden fears, insecurities, anger, sorrow. He prided himself on his ability to hold his emotions back. And suddenly his vulnerable condition left him face to face with raw, overpowering emotions and with no outlet or ready way to express them.

I taught him how to fall apart with dignity. We faced his fears together: wrote about them, talked about them, and, since he couldn't, I danced them for him. We painted his fears and dashed off angry poems. And we cried. A lot. Without shame.

He maintained a positive mental attitude. Perhaps too stiff an upper lip. He was too afraid of his "negative" emotions to let them go completely; this was the legacy of a lifetime of control. But there was emotional movement, and I was happy with all the opening he was able to handle. We did visualizations, but his drawings were weak. He couldn't or wouldn't visualize his cancer as a mad, powerful monster nor himself as an equally fearsome warrior against it. He was caught trying to hold all the pieces of his nice, normal self together while they were being swept out of his fingers by the torrent of this last passage.

He did affirmations, repeating positive thoughts in his head. "From this day on I am no longer ill." "From now on all symptoms and sensations I have are manifestations of recovery." "No matter what else I may be doing, healing is progressing every minute of every day and night." He taped up affirmations all over the house.

As his body declined and his personal well-being grew, we moved more into healing his mind and soul. It was time for the final meeting with his sacred teachers and acknowledging the blessings and wounds he'd received in his life. It was the time to practice the art of detachment.

We began with the root of his life, his mother. Did she love him? Touch him? Know him? Inspire him? Did she have time for him? Take care of him? Treat him with respect and love? For my dad all the answers were no. He was the last of six kids, a change-of-life baby, an accident. He had had to prove to himself and the world that he belonged here, that he had not been a mistake.

I had him write his mother a letter expressing all the feelings he'd choked back all these years. He wrote with tears streaming down his face, as I cradled him in my arms, rubbing his swollen back, as he cried for a mommy he never had. Another day he wrote a portrait of her, distancing himself from her image. Most importantly, we did a meditation during which he discovered her best and worst qualities in himself and made imaginary contact with her, finally releasing her and allowing himself to forgive her. From that day on his sense of responsibility for his own body and confidence in fulfilling its needs and desires became tangibly stronger.

Moving on to his dad was very sad for me. There was little to talk about. His dad didn't know him, didn't touch him, didn't talk to him, didn't know how to love him. My daddy never had a daddy, just a dark cloud who cast a shadow over all his dreams, a grouchy old man who lived to be a hundred. My father wrote his dad an angry letter that arrived at compassion for the old fellow by the end. By the time he wrote a portrait of his dad, he'd become truly detached, and we did a meditation embracing, releasing, and forgiving his father.

Moving on to his relationship with himself, he wrote a brief, but magical autobiography. The story of a farm boy who moved to the big city, got a job, married his true love and had three kids before he was twenty-five. Almost died of cancer at thirty-three. Became a community leader, small-time journalist, sold real estate, settled into a government job for security. A simple man, a simple life.

But his was a life rich in friends and memories. Remarkably, given his childhood, he was a man who'd learned to love, and all that giving was returned by his friends in his last months. For he'd kept the friends he'd had since grade school, since his wedding, since his first job. I ached for and determined to create that sort of continuity in friendship that my uprooted, fragmented, mobile generation hardly knew. He wrote about key moments, like the time his sheep dog Shep got run over, his best friend then, and he couldn't cry—now he did.

We looked back over his life together, at what sort of a parent he'd been to himself. Had he let himself be the person he wanted to be? Had he been his own authority? What did he regret? What did he cherish? We looked at his choices—his mate, his work, the places he chose to live and how he'd fit himself into his world. What kind of husband, what kind of father did he think he was? What kind of employee was he, what kind of boss? We talked about it all. We let go of it all.

And we fed his spirit with rituals, meditations, tapes of sacred music and of spiritual teachers such as Krishnamurti. Having abandoned formal religion at a very early age, he was delighted to find religious teachers whose thought he could respect and identify with. He loved chanting and listening to his loved ones' singing. Sometimes, just my husband, Rob, beating on our trusty heartbeat drum, and me shaking my rattle, both singing his favorite traditional song: "I circle around/ I circle around/ The boundaries of this earth/ Wearing my long-winged feathers/ As I fly/ Wearing...." My dad kept the beat, tapping his bony fingers on my knee.

One day it took him over fifteen minutes to get up out of his favorite chair. "I know what I'm supposed to do. I know I can do it. But I can't find the connection between the two." I knew then we were getting close to the end. My brother and I sat with him, telling him about precious memories. My brother told him, "When I was playing Little League, even on the coldest days, I'd look up in the stands and there you were, Pops. That was so important to me." Every day my mom got him out of bed and dressed him to keep him going. Once, to celebrate his conviction that he was going to make it, we spent our reading hour outdoors amid the buzzing of the bumble bees and the fragrance of fallen peaches. He dozed off in the middle of my reading, and I stared at those features that live on in my own face. I loved the way he looked, and so loved myself in him, recalling John Donne's elegiac lines, "No Spring, nor summer beauty hath such grace,/As I have seen in one autumnal face."

The next day he wasn't able to get up from his bed. I remember the morning as though it were yesterday: The room was flooded with morning sun, but I lit the candles anyway to confirm the light within.

I asked him to feel his spirit in me—in my tones, my rhythms, my gestures, my actions. "See your smile on my face, your wrinkles round my eyes, your long slender fingers on my hands. See your spirit moving through me, through your loving wife, your children, your grandchildren, your family, friends, co-workers, fellow citizens in this state, this country, this world." I guided his spirit through the whole animal kingdom, including his old pal Shep, then the vegetable kingdom, the mineral, and on into space till we stood high on a mountaintop overlooking the entire universe and seeing his spirit in all living things.

Then I called him back to the present moment, focusing on his breathing, his bed, the room, the music, the sounds outside. Suddenly, he sat up and tried to yell, "Hey, everybody, I just went through a rock!" Closing his eyes, he fell back into silence. I watched his breath slowly rising from his belly into his head, and I called each member of the family to spend a few minutes completely alone with him: speaking from their hearts, telling him stories, saying their truth, anything they might be holding onto. I asked my mom to go on in last, and she stayed a long, long time. Then I returned to read to him, to massage his arms and legs and face.

That night, while reading to him, I asked if he remembered our meditation and how he had gone through the rock. He squeezed my hand. I continued to sit with him and to simply hold his hand. After a while he started laughing uproariously and continued to giggle and howl for about ten minutes. It was such a beautiful gift to me, that laughter. Then he fell into silence. Maybe dying wasn't so bad.

About 1:00 A.M. I kissed him and told him I was going to bed. As I left the room, he raised his long freckled arm and waved his final good-bye to me. I stopped in the doorway and looked with bounding love at this wonderful human being who had served me so well.

My mom crawled into bed with him as usual, and I closed the door. At 5:00 A.M. my mother woke me, "Gabrielle, he's gone." He left about 2:00 A.M., the fall solstice. She held him all night, his dead body curled up in her loving arms. No one had ever told her that it takes a few hours for the spirit to leave the body. But her instincts and love taught her.

I didn't spend those months to prove something, but because I had to. They were as vital to me as to my father and family. I tell the story in the hope that it will prove evocative for you.

Here are some exercises to help your appropriation of life's last cycle:

1. Think about and write down how you will relate to loved ones, say, your parents and your mate, as they get older and approach death.

2. How would you like to spend the last cycle of *your* life?

How would you choose to die? What can you do to assure that this happens?

3. Write your epitaph. Write your own eulogy. Write your ethical will—your legacy of wisdom for your survivors.

Life is arranged so that when it's fully lived—the cycles fulfilled—enlightenment comes naturally, inevitably. It is the dynamism of the spirit that carries the whole process along, and it is to the soul's awakening and the spirit's liberation that we now turn.

FOUR
Awakening the Soul
THE POWER OF SEEING

All the world's a stage,
And all the men and women merely players:
They have their exits and their entrances;
And one man in his time plays many parts.

Shakespeare, *As You Like It* (II:7;139)

The fourth shamanic task is to awaken the soul to experience the power of seeing. Seeing the difference between the real and the unreal in ourselves and others. Living from the soul, rather than the ego. Freeing the soul involves living out the authentic roles of the self, our human condition, our mandate: the roles of the dancer, the singer, the poet, the actor, the healer. The diminishing, less-than-human roles that we've learned to adopt over the years out of repressed fear, anger, and sadness are the guises of the ego. We're taught to cast ourselves in small, bit parts, to settle for crummy roles that express only the smallest part of our potential and our soul. Naturally, these ego roles leave us dissatisfied, but we're led to believe by our upbringing and the daily conditioning of society that they are our real selves. We are actors on life's stage. Our challenge is to find the real play, and our *true* roles.

1. SOUL AND THE POWER OF SEEING

Ya' know you'd be o.k., Becky, if you had a self.
So would I. Something to fall back on in a
moment of doubt or terror or even surprise.

From *The Tooth of the Crime*, a play
by Sam Shepard[9]

Our soul, our true self, is the most mysterious, essential, and magical dimension of our being. In fact, it is not a separate reality, as traditional Western thought views it, but the cohesive force that unites our body, heart, and mind. It is not a ghost trapped somehow in the physical machinery of our body, but the very essence of our being.

Each soul is unique, and we are called upon to break out of the minimum security prison of conformity and mediocrity to experience our soul's true magic and power. Our soul is naturally shamanic, the source of all our healing energy. But like a plant it needs to be nurtured to grow and blossom, and to be freed from the entangling, obscuring weeds that tend to take over. The soul is an artist. Its nature is to create, and its natural expression is in the sacred archetypal roles of the dancer, the singer, the poet, the actor, and the healer. Life *is* a cabaret, and our challenge is to act out our essential self on the stage of the world.

Though the soul is not a thing, it is our beingness, that which gives us being. So its presence and absence are visible. Its presence manifests in being awake, attentive, energetic, alive. It is the spark of life. It is absent or dampened when we lack vitality, élan, energy. It is the true self we are seeking in all our explorations, and yet it is not somewhere "out there" but right here now, underneath the false roles we're always casting ourselves in.

Freeing the soul, freeing ourselves to be soulful, means empowering ourselves to really *see* what's going on in ourselves, in others, in our lives. This seeing is not the ordinary sort of looking we're habituated to. Looking operates on the surface; seeing probes beneath to discern the essence, the motion, the energy. Looking is just a matter of regarding things according to our preconceived, static ideas. But as the new physics and biology have clearly shown, our surface impression of the nature of reality as static naively misses the truth of the constant motion and infinite space that truly constitute reality.

Carlos Castaneda, in *A Separate Reality*, gives an arresting example of the difference between seeing and looking. Don Juan describes the death of his son who was crushed by rocks on a highway. "The workers stood around looking at his mangled body. I stood there too, but I did not look. I shifted my eyes so I would see his personal life disintegrating, expanding uncontrollably beyond its limits, like a fog of crystals, because that's the way life and death mix and expand. Had I looked at him I would have watched him becoming immobile and I would have felt a cry inside of me, because never again would I look at his fine figure pacing the earth. I saw his death instead, and there was no sadness, no feeling. His death was equal to everything else." Later he tells Carlos that seeing is "hard work."[10]

Seeing implies detachment. Looking implies attachment. Looking is with the eyes. Seeing is with the whole being. Looking at myself in the mirror, I think that my nose is crooked and too big, my eyes too small, my hair too fine, my hips too wide. I judge. I assess myself by some external criteria that have by now become part and parcel of how I look at people. But if I stare into my left eye in the mirror I see only a still, perfect little doll-like figure of myself in the midst of a deep pool of subtly changing reflections, probably an image much closer to the truth. It is when I can see myself without interpretation that the magic of being, the pure wonder of existing is revealed.

In my workshops I often have the group stand in a circle and ask each person to look at each of the others. I invite the members of the group to notice how each of us is in a body and we are, thus, all very much the same. Each body is born, will die, and on the way will move through many similar stages and circumstances. We share many emotions and needs.

But I then ask them to look round the circle again and to really see each person as an individual with distinct features, shape, tone, energy, attitude. The point is to discover how completely unique each person is. There is no one else, nor has there ever been nor will there ever be, who is exactly like us or any of the people we're seeing.

There is nothing to do about our sameness, except to acknowledge it. Of course, acknowledging it has always been difficult for many of us; all our warlike, racist, sexist, and intolerant behavior throughout history illustrates our constant denial of the simple truth of our essential sameness.

However, our differences are fascinating. They need to be celebrated, explored, expressed. We are each responsible for appropriating our differences and bringing forth our distinctness into the world. No one else has precisely what we have to give. As Hermann Hesse put it, it is "each man's duty to find the way to himself." To one's true self, the soul self.

Appropriating the power of seeing is the deepest of the shamanic tasks we have processed so far. To undertake this phase of the dancing path, we must be willing to let go of everything, including our images, ideas, and beliefs about who we are. We must be willing to die—the death of our ego, which we resist and find as painful as the physical death we fear so much. Most of us are among the walking dead, even though we go around obsessed by a fear of dying, of giving up all that we're attached to. We change nothing, if we can help it. We live in fear of truly being who we are, of living in full 4D, telling the actual truth, dancing our own dance, taking responsibility for transforming our lives into living art. We find all sorts of half-live vocations and preoccupations to avoid the challenge of living life all out as sacred theater.

Life *is* sacred. Life *is* art. Life is sacred art. The art of sacred living means being a holy actor, acting from the soul rather than the ego. The soul is out of space and time and hence always available, an ever-present potential of our being. It is up to each of us to celebrate and to actualize our being, and to turn each meal, conversation, outfit, letter, and so on, into art. Every mundane activity is an opportunity for full authentic self-expression. The soul is our artistic self, our capacity for transforming every dimension of our lives into art and theater.

2. THE SELF AND THE EGO

Human beings are unable to be honest with
themselves about themselves.
Egoism is a sin the human being carries with
him from his birth; it is the most difficult
to redeem. Rashomon *[tried to show]*
the pathetic self-delusions of the ego.

the filmmaker Kurosawa[11]

Our ego holds us back from actualizing our soul in artful living, from turning the pages of our personal history into expressive drama, and celebrating who we really are with daily gusto in our personal style. The ego is often committed to negating our capacity for being, loving, knowing, and seeing. Rather than healing, it can dismember us into a set of minor roles. We tend to take the roles we necessarily play in day-to-day living as the sum and substance of who we are, rather than as disposable character parts that we as sacred actors choose to play as circumstances require.

It is only when we arrive at a profound state of disillusionment that we are ready to begin to investigate the cause of our suffering. My own psychic pain brought me to New York to study with Oscar Ichazo. At the time I seemingly had achieved the American Dream package: an excellent education, travel around the world, marriage to a wonderful man, and success and recognition at an early age. But I was still profoundly unhappy. No amount of sex, money, or power made me feel satisfied and secure. I was suffering chronically and for no apparent reason.

Oscar taught, guided, and goaded me to discover my ego, its various guises, and the potential for soulful living out of the true self behind this ego front. Based on ancient Sufi teachings, Oscar's work probed the structure and workings of the ego, viewing it as psychic armor, a defense system surrounded an exquisite, vulnerable essence.

The ego is a head trip, groups of words that form themselves into repetitive patterns that chatter continuously like crickets in our mind. Oscar taught me how to map these patterns in order to see them in myself and others. And to see beyond them.

It became clear to me that the first stage in self-mastery is determining who we are not. Only then can we be who we are. Likely who you are not is presently who you think you are. That was surely the case for me. I had things inside out: I thought my ego was the real me. "Oh, that's just how I am" was my perennial excuse. When I would repeatedly say, "Well, I'm just not good enough," that really signaled how caught up I was in the rat race, as if I had to constantly prove to myself that I was better than I thought.

In college I learned that I could aggrandize my ego. In life I subsequently learned that the ego sucks the life right out of me. I used to think ego was just a question of vanity, of saying something positive about myself, as if ego could be obviated just by being modest about one's accomplishments.

The facts show that the life of the ego is much more complicated than all that. The ego lives in a state of contradiction and division. It divides us against ourselves. It is the operation of the ego that makes us live in trizophrenia—thinking one thing, feeling another, acting out a third. As I said earlier, I would find myself routinely thinking "yes," feeling "no," and saying "I'll get back to you." Or feeling pissed off, thinking "I'm wrong," and acting polite. Or thinking "I'm cool," feeling insecure, and acting tough. And throughout, being so "self-important," which really means "ego-inflated." As Castaneda's Don Juan puts it, "Self-importance is not something simple and naive.... On the one hand, it is the core of everything that is good in us, and on the other hand, the core of everything that is rotten. To get rid of the self-importance that is rotten requires a masterpiece of strategy. Seers, through the ages, have given the highest praise to those who have accomplished it."[12]

3. THE CHARACTERS IN THE EGO THEATER

Ultimately, the only true power we have is the power to change ourselves for the better. Such change can be an inspiration to others and the greatest gift we can give one another. This is the one great task we can all accomplish: to free the self from being identified with the guises of the ego.

Oscar taught me how to see the difference between my real and my phony self. I began to see what was really happening, and to revision the struggle for my soul in my own terms. My life was a series of cartoon scenes con-

cocted by the ego and quite unconnected with my real
needs and feelings. The ego's characters and plots simply
took on a self-sustaining life of their own.

The key breakthrough for me was the realization that
my ego was comprised of a bunch of desperate characters
that I could name and watch, and begin to see as separate
from my true self. As I began to watch myself, I began to
see that I was not a spontaneous, flexible being able to
respond truthfully in the moment to life's vagaries. Rather,
I found that I was a fixed, repetitive, predictable set of
behavior patterns—psychic tape loops, "numbers" that I
would pull out and repeat over and over again to meet
whatever life offered, whether the routine was appropriate
or not. I lived by cue cards and couldn't respond without
them in even the most ordinary situations; often the cues
were inappropriate, and I ended up befuddled, ineffectual,
and depressed.

The routines were played out in various ways. There
were simple physical habits: I smoked when I was sad,
smoked when I was excited, smoked when I was happy.
There were patterns of emotional repression: I never allowed myself to vent my anger no matter how violated I
felt. And there were recurrent mindsets: for instance, no
matter how complex the circumstances, I always blamed
myself for whatever went wrong.

By paying attention to the daily theater of my ego dra-
mas, I could see my ego directing each play, dragging out
the same old mindsets, prescribing the same routine habits
to go with the same feelings and thoughts. The ego is a
schlock director who knows nothing but clichés, worn-out
routines, and predictable gestures. Each production has all
the freshness of a soap opera rerun.

The more I observed the more I could see that all of my
thoughts, feelings, and actions—no matter how diverse
they might appear—coalesced into three basic patterns. I
had spent most of my life pumping myself up, putting

myself down, and hating myself. The more I could recognize these basic patterns and personalize them into stock characters, the more I gained distance from them. They were over there on the ego stage, and I was over here watching them do their tired routines. Distance provided independence, and they began to lose their hold on me. I no longer identified with them and no longer routinely acted as the characters would have normally had me act. I began to exercise some choice regarding whether I would let this character or that appear: I would ask myself, "Do I really want to do this old number again? Isn't this character boring, or out of place?"

I named the three basic patterns of self-inflation, self-deprecation, and judgment Peter Plan, Norma Nobody, and Judy Judge respectively. These three characters always appear in the same order in the theater of my head. Peter comes on first with his big plans for my destiny; then Norma appears to express despair about ever being able to carry out these grand schemes and collapses into hopeless indolence; and, finally, Judy Judge makes her angry appearance, ripping Norma to shreds for being so wimpy and worthless. So Peter is then spurred on to come up with an even bigger and better plan, and the vicious circle just goes round and round. Thus, not only does the pattern yield a character, but the characters themselves follow a pattern.

My ego's characters are distinct:

Peter Plan is vacuous, abstract, and general. He is ambitious, arrogant, and struts his stuff until he's knocked off his pins and metamorphoses into a timid, insecure, needy shadow of his aggrandized self. He's a charlatan, a fake, a snake-oil salesman, and when he's caught out, he's shown up to be a whimpering, bumbling fool. Peter's like a balloon: he gets all inflated and then is reduced to a piece of limp rubber when punctured.

Norma is never enough: not pretty enough, smart enough, cool enough. She is a black hole without meaning or worth who sucks the life out of everyone else. She's always making fun of herself to confirm her lack of self-worth. Norma fills herself up with everybody else. She's an imitator. She identifies with everyone, because she is no one. She walks, talks, dresses, thinks like somebody else. She reads *People* and Liz Smith to learn about the real people. Norma moves between believing and doubting. She is the perfect seeker: she has no sense of self, so she needs someone to tell her who she is. She whines her way into hopeless despair and wallows in it. Norma is a sloth.

Judy Judge is tense, self-critical, and always to blame. That's why she's always excusing herself: whatever's gone wrong must be her fault; she can't help it. She vacillates between being a puritan and being a hedonist. Constantly criticizing herself, totally preoccupied with her own behavior, she is a sinner full of remorse. That's why she punishes herself, beats herself up. She denies herself until she can't take it anymore, and then abandons herself to any whim, binging on all the pleasure she can find. She breaks the rules, any rules, and then castigates herself for being so wanton.

Peter wants fame. Norma wants love. Judy wants freedom. For all the wrong reasons.

These characters don't perform alone. Each of my mainliners has a cast of supporting characters to manipulate my reality. But they all have one thing in common. They are all phony, just invention intervening between me and the world. Freud adjudged normalcy according to how well people could hold this outer shell together. But I've come to assess psychic health according to how well we can take the shell of normalcy apart.

Everyone has an ego. Everyone has a soul. The struggle between these two forces for control over our lives constitutes our personal story, the story no one else can know. The characters star in our own personal melodrama.

Identifying and separating from the ego is a very theatrical task. The ego can't stand to be exposed, or to be laughed at. That's why we have to pay close attention to capture its personas—their standard lines, habits, costumes, body language—and then blow them up into distinct characters.

We need to summon up the actor within, one of the soul's five authentic ways of worldly expression, to allow us to fulfill this ongoing shamanic task. The first thing an actor has to do is to research the character. In this case, it's a matter of careful monitoring of the self; the more detachment, the more accurate the observation. We have to tune into our inner monologues: they form the subtext of our little melodramas. And we have to listen to our outer voice for the play's set script. If we pay close attention to what we have done in the past and are now doing, what we have said and are now saying, what we have felt and are now feeling, we begin to recognize patterns: the recurrent channeling of our energies, our modes of behavior, and our repetitive plot lines.

Here are some of the inveterate patterns my students have found followed by suggestions for identifying your own:

> I don't do well in groups. I either manipulate to be the center of attention or I drop out to be an observer. It's hard for me to find the middle ground.

> Who said taking responsibility is such a good thing? I don't like it. It takes too much energy to create my own reality. The fact is that I like to feel beleaguered. And if the world disappoints me by not giving me what I need in order to let my shoulder slump and my eyes look resigned, I'll come up with some pretext myself. I'll take

a passing thought—some fantasy of being victimized, like my lover betraying me—and rather than let it slip by, I'll seize upon it and beat myself to a pulp with it. I'll imagine every lurid detail: what he looks like, what a good dancer he is, what she's wearing (or not wearing), what I'll feel like when I find out. I deserve to be pitied.

When attacked, I defend myself with sufficient vigor to cause an attack which allows me to defend with more vigor so as to guarantee a stronger attack which allows me to defend....

I withdraw so I get lonely enough to join long enough to get fed up and withdraw so I can get lonely enough to join....

I resist until I get angry enough with myself to surrender until I get scared enough to resist until I get angry enough to surrender....

And so on through a dozen more Escher-like dog thoughts chasing their tails and tales.

In working to identify the essential dynamic underlying a pattern you've detected, you'll usually find that it comes down to a single gestalt that can be captured in a word or two: victim, liar, superior, spacey. Then, convert that pattern into a person with an apt name.

After working on watching your patterns, cross-examine yourself. Do any of the following characters exist in your life?

EGO CHARACTERS
(not in any particular order of appearance)[13]

Annie Analyze	Norma Nobody	Erotica Velcro
Sissy Spaceout	Fay Fairytale	Dolly Doormat
Sam Star	Darla Desperate	Maria Masochista
I.M. Important	Donna Dumb	I.B. Bland
Judy Judge	Priscilla Perfect	Peter Plan
Brother Superior	Paula Princess	Millie Mystic
Weak Willie	Freddie Flatter	Nellie Needy
Vic Tim	Ida Isolation	Farrah Future
Debbie Deceit	Al Alone	Dougie Druggie
Ronnie Resent	Jill Jealous	Patti Punk
Perry Panic	Eve Ficiency	Arnie Anxious
Defensive Dan	Mary Martyr	D. Presso
Captain Control	Lisa Leftout	Linda Loveless
Harriet Hopeless	Gladys Gorge	Missy Mouse
Harriet Helpless	Tara Tuff	Ivy Envy
Tommy Tuneout	Connie Cling	Ms. Misery
Rita Resistance	Benny Blame	N.L. Retentive

Do any of these lines sound familiar?

"Me first."

"You're wrong."

"Bitch!"

"Can anybody help me?"

"I don't know about you, but I feel great."

"I'm not insecure, am I?"

"Why does this always happen to me?"

"I'll be an artist. No, business is for me. No, I'll stay
    home and cook and sew and have a bunch of kids.
    I don't feel like doing anything."

"Heads I get married, tails I'm gay."

"I'm a piece of shit."

"Notice me! Notice me!"

"I don't feel like it."

"Not now."
"It's all my fault."
"If only I had ..."
"Nobody appreciates me."
"It doesn't matter. It doesn't make any difference."
"Whatever."

There's a character lurking in every line, and every character has standard patter. When you find a character that's yours, examine it under the microscope of truthtelling. Watch how the character moves. Hear what it sings, listen to its lines. What are its entrance cues, what brings this character on stage? Does it appear when you are alone, with a friend, or in a crowd?

Within these three realms of relationship—relationship to self, others, and the world—we have characters that function in each of these domains exclusively and some that operate in all. Some only come out when we're being intimate with someone, and others appear when we're all alone in a room. Others turn on as soon as we go to work. Some show up only in crowds. Some characters go to war, others to church.

Once you have identified a character, play it out to the hilt so that you can see it clearly. Exaggerate it. Flaunt it. This is a game of hide and seek—the ego hiding, the soul seeking. Play out the character's stance, moves, lines, songs. Blow it up. Make fun of it.

Dance the characters, noting where they're comfortable, where they're resistant, where they move and don't, where they're fluid, and where they're stuck. What parts of your body does each character use and what parts doesn't it use? Here are a few of the characters I've seen embodied in people:

Sidney Sniper: feet never far from the ground; spine stiff; legs fluid, head staccato; he slides and snaps, jaw tight, radar on, every movement calculated.

Norma Nobody: shoulders slumped; head and hands hunched forward; face dull; chest sunken; she moves with heavy, indolent effort.

Oral Robert: all mouth; tongue, teeth, and jaw in constant motion; staccato activity from hand to mouth; he cracks his gum, slurps his coffee.

Nellie Needy: sucks in energy with her begging eyes, solicitous words; limp, supplicant body language.

Priscilla Perfect: tight ass and pursed lips.

Captain Control: shoulders up; knees tight; pelvis locked; jaw shut; elbows in; he doesn't breathe below the neck.

Your characters have their songs and music too. Singing is a delightful way to explore and express a character you've uncovered. They have their distinctive lyrics and styles (country, blues, operatic, punk rock, etc.). Have you met Valerie Victim? When she gets in my way, I sing her song:

The Blame Game
(music: walking bass; snapping fingers)

My hair is too thin,
My nose too long,
God fucked me up,
He made me wrong.
I've had trouble since I grew up;
It's not my fault, my parents screwed up.

chorus:

It's all your fault;
It's all her fault;
It's all his fault;
It's all their fault.

If I lose my job,
Or they raise the rent,
I curse out loud

At the President.
My lover says I'm too uptight,
But the bed's too hard, and the light's not right.
chorus

The drummer in the band is off tonight;
I could dance real well if the music were right.
I would've been happy from the day I was born,
If Mars hadn't been in Capricorn.

I wrote this country and western tune to capture Norma Nobody's prolonged puberty. Try it with a loopy melody and a big twang:

I've given this body to folks
I wouldn't even loan my car;
I've had every infection, including rejection,
Every drug from acid to booze.
I've done it to music
In cars, on the floor
Lord,
There's got to be more....

Why not make up a few more verses for her?
You can rap out a whole series of characters in pieces like "The Character Rap" by Fun Kee:

chorus:

And the circle turns and the circle spins
Such tight little patterns we live within.

Sam the Star in the spotlight,
He's got a need to be seen that's outasight.
He thinks he's owed something special from the
*   universe*
And when it doesn't come, well then things get worse,
Because Bob Abused, the Victim Man
Slides on the scene just as quick as he can.
He moans and groans and wimps along

Till he finally gets pissed that he's treated so wrong.
And when he's pissed, Sidney Sniper knows what it's
        all about;
He don't take no shit, he dishes it out.

chorus

Captain Control is an angry dude;
He struts around with an attitude.
He barks and shouts to keep everything straight.
And God forbid he should ever be late,
Because Arnie Anxious would lose his grip
Or Paul Pout would drop his lip,
        Would drop his lip, would drop his lip.
And then Norma Nobody would give up her space
To hold Paul's hand or stroke his face;
Sweet Norma is a mask for Ronnie Resent
Who always holds on to what she shoulda spent
Instead of letting it out, she just takes more in
As Gladys Gorge on an eating binge,
Until Priscilla Perfect stops the eating trip
With her little tight ass and her tight little lips.

chorus

There's Fay Fairytale, she just wants to dance
With hopes and dreams and a lot of romance
So that Paula Princess can stay on the shelf
Without lifting a finger to help herself.
But who fights the hardest to grab the brass ring—
A sticky, gooey lady called Connie Cling,
        Called Connie Cling, called Connie Cling.

chorus

Brother Superior is a spiritual guy;
His pants have strings, but his shoes don't tie.
He doesn't like the world; he doesn't think he fits.
So he hides from it all behind Nick Noncommit,
Who won't make up his mind for this or for that.

To him the status quo is where it's at.
But when he finally chooses to take a stand,
He moves in the clothes of Peter Plan.
Peter has the future right in his hands,
But each plan only leads to another plan,
    To another plan, to another plan.

chorus

Here comes Patti Punk, all scowls and fists,
But it's only at herself that she ever gets pissed.
She hates herself; she thinks she's shit.
So she turns to Harriet Hopeless as a mainline hit.
Harriet always fails and Harriet always quits.
Her psyche sags like an old lady's tits.
Harriet is a lady with defeat on her mind,
Not like Sissy Spaceout whose mind you can't find.
Sissy thinks that life is a magazine,
Until Judy Judge interrupts her dream.
Judy looks at life as right or wrong;
To tell you the truth, she probably hates this song.

And the circle turns and the circle spins
Such tight little patterns we live within.

As you do this character work, you are mapping your
ego. First you chart the characters themselves: who they
are, how they move, feel, act. Most importantly, how they
think, what they say. The characters in the plays of our ego
are rich material for self-revelatory poetry, prose, monologue. Characters like Patti Punk with her punk poetry:

I used to take speed;
I was in a hurry to die;
I can't remember why.
Movin' in the fast lane,
Tryin to beat the pain
With little round pills,
Dressed to kill

In aqua blue dye,
They made me high,
They made me high.
I used to take speed;
I was in a hurry to die;
I can't remember why.

Or Robert Dinero:

Let me give it to you straight. Making money is
just a game. And I love to play it, because it brings out
the best in me. Money's the best game in town. I control
my wife with it. I relate to my kids and run their lives
through it. I prove my manhood with it. I accumulate
power with it. True, I beat the shit out of myself for
not having enough of it, and I worry and think and
analyze about it instead of myself. But, boy, when I'm
raking in the dough, I'm in heaven, and I don't give a
damn about anything else.

Or Erotica Velcro (Connie Cling's identical twin):

Save me!
Take me!
Buy me!
Show me!
Feed me!
Need me!
Love me!
Fuck me!
Protect me!
Marry me!

Or Rita Resistance:

I carry my resistance with me wherever I go. I bury
my treasures and lose the map. I knot my frustrations
and bind my feelings into sweet little bows. I'm doing
time in an antique lace prison, serving my sentence

in a crushed velvet cell. I am a prisoner, weaving my own web of solitary confinement.

We have to continue to probe deeper and deeper. Where do we get stuck? What are our psychic routines? We have to keep our antennae tuned for the ego's appearances, keep unearthing new characters, hearing their voices:

Bonnie Bulimia (and her twin Annie Rexia):

I stuff. I starve. I blow up. I throw up. I know the exact location of every 24-hour market within a ten-mile radius. I don't care about food; I'm just obsessed with it. I hide apples in my closet and wolf down desserts in the middle of the night. I know the caloric content of everything from ice cream to cucumbers. I fast. I starve. I live on liquid protein and faint in airports. I am a starving woman.

Sidney Sniper:

Anger is my ammunition. I've been storing it up for years, never wasting it in the moment, but lying in wait for the time to strike. I like to take my enemy by surprise. My weapons are words—big ones, little ones. Words that can really hurt or merely sting. I can drop them like bombs or sharpshoot with pinpoint accuracy. Sometimes I fire before I'm attacked: a preemptive strike, an aggressive defense keeps people at a distance, where they can't hurt me.

Captain Control:

I learned that the only way to be with people was not to be with them. To be in control. To be special, be the best. Achievement, that will get me what I need. So I compete and compare with conceit and flair. I compete and compare with deceit and despair. I'm not with you unless I compete—that's my deceit. I don't

see you unless I compare—that's my despair. What
I end up with is what I started with, nonstop achieve-
ments that never satisfy.

Some characters function in the past, some in the future, others more or less in the present. But they all function to keep us out of the moment, out of what is really
going on. What is the tense of your inner monologue, what
you're always saying to yourself? In general, my ego lives
in the past—rehashing old scripts, sometimes reworking
them, digging up old memories to prove my lack of self-
worth, reinforcing my deep-seated sense of blame and failure. My ego's characters are always punishing me, deriding
me, putting me down in one way or another, smothering
my self in opprobrium.

Other egos live in the future, always two steps ahead of
themselves. They're getting ready for what's coming rather
than experiencing what is. They back into parking spaces,
thinking about leaving as they arrive. Or, they prepare
themselves for the worst so it won't hurt so much when
life disappoints them.

And there are those who simply occupy the present
with self-absorption and self-consciousness, as they worry
about how they look, what they're saying, how to be, who
to be (or not to be).

Watch where your inner chatter spends the most time
in hashing, rehashing, shaping, and reshaping your life.

Everyone has an ego. You, me, your mother, father,
everyone else you know. Some egos are preoccupied with
sex, others with money, some with power. Some are loners,
some constantly need someone, anyone, and others are
groupies. Some live in deceit, always lying to themselves
and others. Some are totally lazy about taking care of their
own needs. Some are so scared to do anything that they
end up doing nothing but spinning their wheels. Some
identify with everything and everyone. Others justify their

every action. And some consider, weigh, analyze every move. Some are gluttonous, some vain, others stingy or depressed or excessive or cowardly or envious.

The ego in its various guises reacts; it has no real creative power to initiate anything. Rather, it clicks into its routine when set off, like an answering machine that carries different messages and different styles at different times.

In working on the ego, it's good to work with the exercises suggested in the previous chapter on the life cycles. You'll find that the raw material for your character's attitudes, monologues, and styles comes from the early stages of your life. The ego develops at a tender age in moments of doubt, terror, or deceit. There the patterns begin. Early on we stop responding to life in a spontaneous and open way and begin to construct our defenses against it. The formational events need not be traumatic to be pivotal, but they can be recalled as vivid turning points. You would do well to search your life for such turning points in the development of your ego and its characters.

Here are a few workshop participants' memories of their ego development:

My first day at school the teacher asked what our fathers did for a living. The other kids said construction worker, fireman, waiter, and so on. So I said mine was a plumber. Actually he was a doctor. He was amazed when later he saw his occupation on my school records. When he asked me why I lied, I said that I just wanted to fit in.

———

I remember being five years old and playing in my sandbox, building the most beautiful castle. "Mom, Dad, come see my beautiful castle." But they never came. That's when the campaign to win their attention began. "Mom, Dad, come see me be president of my

class; come see me be high school valedictorian; come
see me graduate summa cum laude from Harvard; Mom,
Dad, come see me be a successful doctor; come see my
beautiful house; come see my beautiful blonde girl
friend."

———————

I was playing basketball in the driveway when my
dad drove up. I was eager to see him because I was finally
able to make a basket. I said, "Hey, Dad, look at me,"
and slipped one right through the net. He said, "Yeah,
but can you do it with your left hand?"

In such little moments is the ego unconsciously born
and nurtured. The patterns begin, the circles spin, and
there's no way out but through. The patterns become in-
grained, and they don't go away with wishing or neglect.
The struggle between the ego and the soul continues
throughout life. The work of disentangling ourselves is hard
and serious. Once you get into it, it's amazing to see how
strong a grip these characters have on our psyches. Just as
you see a pattern and begin to separate yourself from it by
turning it into a character, you find yourself doing and
saying the same things, except in a new context and costume.

One workshop participant identified his principal ego
character as Sam Star:

I've always performed to get attention and love. I've
always struggled to be seen. As a financier, I loved being
seen as the one with the answers, the one who could
handle any situation, the one who performed the financial feats. And when I gave it all up, I loved being seen
as the guy who could give it all up. Now I'm doing
photography and I want what I see to be seen ... the
struggle never ends; it just changes form.

Other long-time students have identified the merry-go-round the ego keeps riding as it shifts from character to character. Here's a sample analysis:

> First, there's Defensive Dan. Whenever I'm approached from outside, he's the first guy out of the gate, even if he has to make up some attack to justify his appearance.
>
> From Defensive Dan I usually spin into Weak Willie. This guy's terrific—he's got a bad back, tired muscles, doesn't get enough sleep. He feeds on pity.
>
> When Weak Willie goes all the way he becomes my victim character, Bob Abused. This is my main man. I'd love to give him a rest, because he puts in so much overtime.
>
> When Bob Abused goes all the way he heads toward Martin Martyr; but Bob never goes all the way down.
>
> He eventually takes that negative energy, transmutes it, and becomes Sidney Sniper—a mean, vengeful, deceitful, stealthy character who'll lash out at you. And often his attacks provoke counterattacks that bring on guess who? Good old Defensive Dan again.
>
> I watch my stored-up feelings pour into these guys: my sadness into Bob Abused; my fear into Weak Willie and Al Alone; my anger into Defensive Dan and Sidney Sniper.
>
> And the psychic gerbils keep going around and around in their cages.

The psychic energy and wasted intellectual power all this takes is startling. No wonder we only live at a fraction of our capacity, since so much of our energy and talents are taken up with this pointless melodrama.

Even once we're attuned to the tricks of the ego, we have to work to maintain our center, to act from the still-point of our true self. The characters are always lurking around the corners of our minds ready to seduce us into their little scenes. We find ourselves musing for a moment about, say, a budding relationship, and all of a sudden we're embroiled in our own version of *The Days of Our Lives*:

Ida Isolation: I'm lonely.

Ivy Envy: I wish I had a relationship that was totally balanced like Sam and Jessica. I wonder if she gets jealous.

Jill Jealous: I can't stand it when other women grab my man's attention.

Vicki Victim: And he gives it to them just to hurt me, and I don't even do anything wrong.

Cathy Competition: In fact, I'm always more beautiful than they are. I mean the last one he was out with had ugly, frizzy hair and big thighs. Just thinking about him makes me realize...

Paula Pride (interrupting): I don't need him. I can walk on my own two feet. He can do whatever the hell he wants.

Debra Deceit: I mean, I really don't care that much about our relationship. I'm much happier with a bunch of lovers.

Anna Lyze: I've got it all figured out. If he were to be more multidimensional, then I could fulfill all the facets of my personality. I'm only interested in having affairs with other men because they satisfy needs that he's not meeting. I think analysis would be good for him, since it's clear he hasn't got in touch with his oedipal complex. On the other hand...

Eve Efficiency: I think it would be best for me to go all the way into my independence and create my life alone. I'll begin in the mornings playing the tamboura. That's at 7:30. After that, I shower, eat breakfast, then go to the studio. Let's see. Afternoons I'll spend two hours on

the flute, one hour doing aerobics. I'll get home in time
for dinner at 6:00 and the national news at 7:00. Oh, I
should schedule fun at least one night a week. Oh, and
on Thursdays and Sundays I'll make love.

Farrah Future: And then when I'm together and on my
own, that's when the right man for me comes along.
The man I'm supposed to be with. I'll attract him.

Patsy Panic: But what if I don't? What if I have to stay
with this one, and have all the pressure on me to make
it work?

Betty Bitch: Then I'm stuck with him, and he's frightening. He's messy, uncouth, secretive, stingy, misery
to be around. He gets honey all over the counters and the
refrigerator handle, never picks up after himself, he's
loud, he's a creep!

Rita Regret: Oh, why am I such a bitch? Why do I
compete? I wish I didn't analyze the relationship and
judge him. And why do I lie to myself? I almost don't
care.

Ms. Misery: This life isn't worth living. Living with
him is like living on a roller coaster ride. One minute
he's up and I'm down; the next, he's down and I'm up.
We're never in the same place at the same time. Is this
any way to live? I may as well live alone.

Ida Isolation: But I'm so lonely....

Characters also move from one extreme to the other—
from puritan to hedonist, from feeling superior to feeling
inferior, from being a true believer to being fraught with
doubt. The ego actually caricatures our true self: it presents us to the world as either a tough dude or totally dumb,
as affectionate as a puppy or as aloof as a coyote, as pushy
and aggressive or pulled back and indifferent. We're swung
violently back and forth between these cartoon versions of
ourselves and between this drama and what's true. It's no

wonder that so often we feel ill at ease, being so regularly diminished and misrepresented by the metamorphoses of our ego.

What we really need and want, of course, is not to be directed but to direct our life in an authentic and genuinely satisfying way. Doing this character work on flushing out and defusing the power of the ego—after experiencing freedom in our body, expression in our heart, and dynamic stillness in our mind—enables us to see the contour and content of our ego, the fixed forms our unconscious mind takes. We need to cultivate that stillpoint at the center of ourselves, the steady witness, the soul of attention and intention, as distinct from the ephemeral appearances and petty plots of the ego. Each one of us is the one who is watching and as the watcher we each ultimately have the power to choose who to be.

4. Enacting the Soul

To confront a person with his shadow is to show
him his own light.

Carl Jung[14]

The seed of the ego's tight grip on our psyche takes root in our unconsciousness, in our lack of awareness of its routines. Seeing how our ego operates gives us the option of using its characters, or being used by them. The self needs to direct the play of our life. Our potential, our vision, our story is bigger than the TV shows the ego casts us in. It is high time to call upon the actor dimension of our soul, our sacred capacity for both being oneself and watching oneself at the same time.

The soul is a holy actor,* a true whole self in action. The challenge of enlightened living is not to achieve tranquility

*I first came across this term in *Towards a Poor Theater* by Jerry Grotowski.

in monastic solitude, but to enact one's true self in the day-to-day world. We need to become actors in the theater of daily living, consciously aware of what we're doing. Actors who recognize in our breathing, our movements, our human contact, the obstacles blocking our instinctive responses to life. The goal of the shamanic actor is to be free and spontaneous, physically, emotionally, and mentally, in order to be totally appropriate and present in the moment. This kind of actor is a dancer, singer, poet, all in one gesture, tone, and thought, easing effortlessly into each present moment, each shifting scene.

Enacting our soul means creating a fresh self, an ever-changing yet enduring self, that can play any role, take any position—with full awareness and control. That is the difference between the soul and the ego. The soul plays the self as a consummate stage actor plays a character—with detachment and total involvement at the same time.

The characters of the ego are necessary to move through the daily rituals of life. We have to take on various guises, various roles. The key is not to become lost in the ego's roles, to identify the self with them, but to enter and then drop them when necessary and appropriate, even just for fun and delight. Most social interaction takes place at the level of the ego, and we have to play some role or other. To function effectively we have to play the game, but in order not to lose our soul we have to realize it is merely a game, and choose when and how to play it.

The holy actor sees, and then uses, characters in the theater of life. He is the criminal defense lawyer who consciously uses Bob Abused, Sidney Sniper, and Sam Star to win his case. Or the lover who indulges Fay Fairytale without drowning in her sentimentality and attachments. Or the artist who uses Judy Judge to evaluate her work, but not to rip it apart. It's me when I use Peter Plan to schedule my workshops, as long as I don't take him with me. With detachment and practice you will find the appropriate times and places to let your ego characters have their hour upon the stage.

Once you really get into this character work, you will begin to see your soul. It is the part of you that danced, sang, and wrote its way through this book, and then came into full flower in this chapter.

As a holy actor you need inspiration. This is a healing process, a gathering of forces, a unifying of energy into a dynamic harmony. It is not easy to reverse the process of normal conditioning and release your soul to direct your ego. It takes a warrior. As Carlos Castaneda puts it in *The Fire From Within*: "A warrior is self-oriented, not in a selfish way, but in the sense of a total and continuous examination of the self."[15] A warrior is committed to the spiritual path, the path charted by great myths and religious traditions, the map to the stillpoint that is the axis of all authentic movement.

The ego reacts. The soul responds. The soul responds in innocence, love, serenity, humility, truth, courage, detachment, equanimity, sobriety, and integrity. Our authentic roles in life are not the bit parts of the ego's melodramas, but the archetypes of the soul: our most essential, vitalizing calling is to be dancer, singer, poet, actor, and healer. The soul enacts these qualities in creative interplay with oneself, others, and the world. And it opens the way for a life grounded in the spirit.

FIVE

Embodying the Spirit

THE POWER OF HEALING

Shamanism = technique of ecstasy.

Mircea Eliade[16]

The fifth shamanic task is to embody the spirit in order to experience the power of healing. Healing, making whole, the self and all that the self involves: one's body, heart, mind, soul, and spirit.

To the extent that our spirit remains dormant and uncatalyzed, buried within us as pure potential, we operate at the level of inertia; when our spirit fills us to overflowing we are in ecstasy. Freeing the spirit means being able to move from inertia to inspiration through the steps of imitation, intuition, and imagination. The dancing path is in essence an ongoing, ever-new journeying from inertia to ecstasy. And as our lives become more and more spirit-filled, we reach the level of ecstasy more and more readily. Ecstasy becomes our natural state of being: vibrant, attentive, still within, flexible without, joyous beyond joy. As the life cycles mapped our external journey from birth to death, the spiritual layers chart our inner journey from death to rebirth, from sleepwalking existence to being totally awake.

Our body, heart, and mind, alone or unified as soul, mark us as distinct from all other living beings. Our spirit is that dimension of ourselves that connects us to the whole. Our spirit is our share in the energy that "moves the sun and other stars," that charges everything with movement and potency. As Gary Zukav in *The Dancing Wu Li Masters*, Fritjof Capra in *The Tao of Physics*, and several other scientists have shown, everything in the universe, down to the most "inanimate" object, is at its core filled with movement and space.

More and more the worldviews of advanced physics, chemistry, and astronomy parallel those of traditions such as Buddhism and, in effect, the esoteric core of all the great traditions. We find that the deeper we probe the matter of creation the more we bump up against the mystery of non-matter, uncreated energy, infinity. In a word, spirit. As the Hasidic masters taught, the spark of the infinite that energizes each of us derives from the same ultimate source. We needn't interpret this source theistically, but it is easy to think of it as a universal energy in which everything participates to some degree. Hence, freeing the spirit means fanning that spark of infinity into a consuming fire, channeling the ultimate into the now, embodying the infinite in our finite lives. All of a sudden, from this point of view, all the ecstatic utterances of the mystics begin to make sense.

At one point late in his too short life, the Trappist monk Thomas Merton fell madly in love with a woman who'd nursed him while he was in the hospital. This love disrupted all monkish conventions, but Merton was then open to experiences, to politics, to thoughts, to love that went beyond conventional bounds. Still, he had to struggle mightily with the conflict between his religious vows and his soaring desires. When he asked a former novice what he should do, the man, who had gone back to Nicaragua to become a politically active priest and a renowned poet, replied, "Follow the ecstasy."

The challenge, of course, is to discover wherein true ecstasy lies and how to follow it. For, obviously, ecstasy isn't simply infatuation, titillation, some temporary high that comes through drugs, ephemeral achievement, etc. Such things are simply intimations, if not imitations, of ecstasy. Rather, ecstasy means being fully alive.

The path to ecstasy is up through the five layers of consciousness, the five levels through which energy most naturally flows from purely physical existence to its highest spiritual potential. The layers afford a revelatory angle from which we can view our selves, our relationships, our personal history, the organizations we're involved in, the ebb and flow of daily life, etc.

The first layer is *inertia*, the level of nonmovement and total "unconsciousness." Many people "live" and die holding onto all of their energy, never getting anything moving, and without any exploration of themselves and their potential. This is the frightened, passive, vegetative state of the perennial wallflower, victim, cog in the wheel.

There's a way out of this static state. Sooner or later, some way of living, or some person, catches our attention as representing a richer, more desirable possibility for ourselves, and we are catalyzed into the layer of *imitation*. We join a religious order, go to law school, study dance, follow a guru, take on a mentor. Imitating another person, following an external form allows us to move out of inertia into energizing movement.

But imitation has its obvious shortcomings. We cannot express our full, true selves by simply following another person or a set of external guidelines and ideals. When the limitations and staleness of imitation begin to constrict our need for our own voice, our own style, our own way, we need to take the plunge into *intuition*—to venture beyond the safe childhood patterns of following others' leads and feel our own way into the chaos of personal creativity.

Intuition, if it is to be truly fruitful, has to eventually emerge from the welter of creative anarchy into the ordered creativity of what Northrop Frye calls "the educated imagination." The next layer of consciousness, imaginative creativity, puts us into expressive form, but it is now our own distinctive, unique form. *Imagination* marries our physical, emotional, and mental energies into a dynamic harmony that allows for spontaneous and appropriate expressiveness. Imaginative living means acting creatively and without attachment in each situation that arises. It is at the level of imagination that we understand life as theater and our personality or ego as simply a series of characters we each play. We become the conscious director of these characters as we engage with freedom and integrity in life's multiple scenes.

Beyond imagination lies the level of *inspiration* in which we transcend conscious effort, and begin to design and operate with spontaneous creativity out of our spiritual center. We live on an inspired, ecstatic level—our moving, our singing, our writing, our acting—all our training and discoveries coming through effortlessly, and unselfconsciously.

It's easiest, of course, to see these five levels of consciousness specifically in artistic expression. Imagine, for instance, the stages in the development of a virtuoso violinist. He starts at zero (usually as a child) with nothing but potential—his hands, heart, and mind completely incapable of making music on the instrument. Then perhaps he hears some fantastic violinist playing and is moved to try to learn. He finds a teacher, listens to great players, and, eventually, after a long period of time, learns how to play the classical repertoire with fidelity and precision. Then he searches to find his own unique style, *his* distinct expression; he may break with his teacher, violate conventional interpretations, flout the rules, or, less disruptively and more gradually, just develop his own musical expression. And when he marries these intuitive explorations with the legitimate demands of musical scores, collaboration with orchestras, etc., he's able to make distinctive imaginative contributions to our musical experience. If he's blessed, there will then be more and more occasions in which the whole project of creative production recedes into the background—technique, scores, conductors, studios, audiences—and the playing becomes everything.

But the journey from inertia to ecstasy is not just for artistic geniuses. It is the natural birthright of each one of us. In fact, through this book, you have already started down the dancing path from inertia to ecstasy. On this road to your full, true self, the rhythms are your tools, the core feelings your allies, the life cycles your vehicle, the sexual stages your driving force, and the character work your roles and scripts.

1. INERTIA

The first layer of consciousness, then, is inertia. It is a level of nonmovement; it is a level in which your energy, whether on the dance floor or in your psyche, is simply stuck.

Everybody experiences inertia. It is the groggy, barely conscious state when you first wake up in the morning. Or when you return to work from vacation. Or when you are in momentary insecurity about something or other. It is the state of despairing inaction when you've been profoundly disappointed or the numbed catatonia of being locked into the same routine day after day. The drugged passivity of TV watching. The stoned immobility of drug-taking, drinking. The moral and intellectual laziness of just getting by.

The only question is whether you choose to live in inertia or pass through it in the flow of your life—day to day, year to year, cycle to cycle. Inertia is seductive. It has the characteristics of the ecstasy we're seeking and knew in the womb. It's natural, effortless, totally accommodating. But we're made to move, to become, to grow, to change, to create, and the true paradise of ecstasy lies not in inaction but in action that is so totally absorbing it seems like no work at all. All too quickly the false ecstasy of lazing around, indulgence, and passivity takes its toll in the self-destructive effects of imploded energy.

Anyone who has gotten into running or aerobic exercise of any sort knows the experience of having to break out of inertia. There's always some reason for not running, not exercising. And even when you do, initially it feels terribly hard, uncomfortable, unrewarding, a pointless self-punishment. You suspect that you were right all along in thinking all those joggers and jazzercise people were just egotistical masochists. But gradually exercise begins to feel more and more natural, just what the body was designed to do. Eventually you can become more and more expressive and creative in exploring your body's potential and experience longer and longer stretches of pure physical joy, when running or exercising is no longer a conscious effort but a completely natural dynamic way of being, like a deer or a cheetah that runs many miles a day with grace and élan.

As a temporary resistance to the demands of life, inertia is simply a place from which to start. As you recognize its grip on you, you can confront it with movement and vitalize your being with the energy of change. You can summon the dancer within, the part of you that instinctively knows how to explore the full range of the body's rhythms. It is natural for the body to move, and the simplest way out of inertia is to start moving it. Stretch, lean, shuffle, swirl, with or without music, alone or with others.

The easiest way is just to ease into flowing movements that will gradually seduce the body into the other rhythms. Dance is always available no matter where you are and is a ready catalyst to get your energy moving.

If you live in inertia—"waking sleep," Gurdjieff called it—as your basic energy level, as most of us do, your reality is comprised of a structure of unquestioned beliefs and frozen attitudes which are a bulwark against change. Movement and change are feared as painful and disruptive. The status quo seems to offer a haven of security. Truthfully, you're a wallflower at the dance of life, refusing every offer to move, out of fear of the unknown or of making a fool of yourself; you don't make the effort. But this holding back—hanging on tight to everything, especially your body, which becomes the repository of all your repressed feeling, thoughts, and action—uses up all your physical, emotional, and mental energy. And there is nothing to show for this utilization of your energy but the same old patterns and a deteriorating body and spirit. Because you don't dare to breathe life in and let it out, you live on a very restricted energy supply.

At bottom, inertia is the level of being unconscious, the home of the victim, the place where life just happens to you and you're unaware of your responsibility to create your own reality. It's the level of the pregnant woman who obliviously chainsmokes, the macho laborer who stupefies himself every night with a six-pack, the high-powered executive who's married to his job and measures everything and everyone, including himself, by company standards, or the actor who has nothing to say without a script.

In inertia we want our life and friends to be stable, predictable, homogenized. It's so much easier to be in control when things around us don't change and we have the security of the known. We stay in an unhappy marriage or job or situation for years and years rather than risk the uncertainty, the adventure, the pain of venturing forth. In fact, all our "adventure" is planned and prepackaged, innocuous and ultimately dissatisfying—we buy the hype of cruises, cars, beer, movies, to sate our frustrated desire for true novelty and authentic experience.

Often we turn around and watch even our children lock themselves into routines and perspectives that suffocate them, choke their growth and spontaneity, and snuff out the sparks we saw burning in each of them when they first entered the world. It hurts as we watch them lock into the vicious spiral of victimization, resentment, isolation. Or of flattery, melancholy, and self-importance. We know the dances all too well. We taught them the steps. We reinforce these patterns rather than acknowledging our children's pain and guiding them to face the challenges that will nurture their growth. Because we are not bold, not warriors, we don't empower our children—to their lifelong detriment. Seeing their weakness, cowardice, and compromising is to watch parts of ourselves die, the parts that are young and fresh and full of promise.

Listen to the voices of inertia: Don't rock the boat. You're making a big mistake. Don't act impulsively. You've got to plan ahead. Be careful. Be prepared. But think of your family. Think of your friends. But if you do that.... Don't burn your bridges. You'll regret it. You'll be sorry.

2. IMITATION

Imitation may be faint praise, a timid venture, but it is the vital first step in escaping the grip of inertia. It is the level of psychic development in which you strive for something more in your life and allow yourself to pay attention to your own growth. Even if it is just admiring someone else's steps, getting turned on by a book, a lecture, a movie, or yearning for something just hinted at, the reaching out sets you on a road of discovery, a path of adventure. You make something happen, you start moving in the direction of life. The couch potato life of the conventional, the expected, the easy is now history. You're on your way.

The form may be physical or mental, aerobics or philosophy. It may be for healing or pleasure, therapy or dancing. It may be authoritarian or democratic, the army or a country club. It may be rigid or loose, ballet or jogging. It may be individual or collective, yoga or zen. It can be artistic, religious, educational, or political. You may stay in one form or move through many. You may end up with an alligator on your shirt, a feather in your hair, or a shaved head. It doesn't matter. All forms are functional. They are stepping stones to substance, an opportunity to learn to surrender. Imitation is a vital part of your path, a way to learn, a catalyst for change. It eases you out of inertia by presenting a precise picture of what is expected of you and the exact way to realize that expectation. Whether you're a sannyasin, a budding figure skater, a future farmer of America, or an aging seminarian, following a teacher through a proven set of steps gets you moving in the direction of spiritual liberation.

The key is not to get stuck in imitation, not to believe that taking the well-trod path and following the rules is the aim of spiritual development. Often the spiritual ideal that is held out requires absolute observance of the rules, total surrender to the master, immersion into a way of life. But imitation is the childhood of spiritual growth, the first steps out of inertia. Just as in childhood you learn to relate to someone outside of yourself, so on the level of imitation you expand beyond yourself and your inaction in order to engage teachers and new ways that evoke and channel your potential.

All spiritual ways are not equal. The most expansive are those that involve your whole self, not just a piece or one dimension of yourself, and provide a context for your growth rather than just a picture of it. Also, all ways don't work for all people. Not eating meat is an authentic spiritual practice, but not if you are an Eskimo whose body needs meat to survive. Some ways possess the vitality of living, nurturing, and inexhaustible source; others are bound by the ego, vision, and charisma of their creators; still others have become desiccated shells held rigidly in place by timid, weak-souled disciples who make an airtight system out of the founder's fresh, responsive teaching and dare not, often cannot, bring the teaching to new life in the present moment. Whatever path you choose, it can become part of your own dancing path only if you don't identify with it as the ultimate expression of your spiritual development.

Identifying totally with one specific way is not spiritual freedom, but imprisonment. You can't see beyond it. You make the teacher into a god, the teaching absolute truth, and end up unable to see the value and meaning of anything else. It becomes, as Doris Lessing puts it, "a prison we choose to live in."[17] And so many of us end up simply transferring from one prison to another—each in turn becoming intolerable—without seeing that we are locking ourselves into believing each way as absolute. A particular system can take over your persona: you start dressing, speaking, and acting like its charismatic leader; you eat, drink, and sleep the system. Rather than being a path to somewhere else, it becomes an end. Rather than enhancing your own unique life, it becomes a way of life to which you subsume your unique self.

It's so easy to become, rather than use, the form. If someone asks you who you are, and you reply, "I'm an editor"; "I'm a lawyer"; "I'm a runner"; "I'm a photographer," then you've functionally limited your self, your being, to a certain role, a certain activity. Or to say "I'm a Scientologist" or "I'm a Rajneeshee" or "I'm a Catholic" or "I'm a vegetarian" is to restrict your potential to some limited, if valid, perspective.

On the dancing path, the level of imitation exists to catalyze change. Imitation starts us moving out of inertia. By first following someone else's steps, we are coaxed, jolted, or seduced out of stasis by a vision, a possibility, an ideal that speaks to our deeper aspirations. The danger is that the way—law, yoga, dance, religion, etc.—itself becomes a kind of institutionalized inertia in which you get trapped. You may see the system as having all the answers, satisfying all your needs, defining all the meaning and value in your life, or settling once and for all who you are. But any way that doesn't keep you on the edge, keep you moving and growing and changing, is not really a way, but a trap. Your freedom from inertia becomes short-lived, and your growth dies an early death, even if it seems you're living a totally involving life.

Security is the ego's holy grail. A way designed to be a catalyst for growth easily can become a cover for inertia. The idealistic novice, eager to dedicate herself to a worthwhile cause and a spiritual flowering, soon submerses herself in the roles of superobserver of the rules, mother superior's little helper, etc.; the enthusiastic disciple becomes a clone of the master, with no style, no ideas, and no identity of his own; the budding ballerina learns how to make all the moves, how to look, how to conform to the imperious teacher's aesthetic demands; the crusading law student kowtows to the cynical wisdom of her elders and becomes "realistic" about the legal system and its rewards for those who play it right. If you don't have a strong sense of yourself, you can unconsciously cover up your lack by immersing yourself in a relationship to a method or an organization. If you don't know how to relate to society and the universe—if you can't find your place—then a system, a group, or a career can give you a definitive, off-the-rack answer.

Organizations are anxious to define our identities, our role, our place in the scheme of things. But the psychic wounds of undeveloped instincts don't become healed by immersion in systems that protect you from having to confront them.

I always know I'm in the imitation mode when I hear the voice of self-consciousness turn on in my head: Am I doing this right? Are they looking at me? Why are they looking at me? I bet they're laughing at me. They all know. Know what? Know I don't know. I feel like such a jerk. Is my hair all right? How am I supposed to dance to this music?

Or I think about somebody copying me. Copying my style. Wearing my expressions on their face. Taking my ideas. Adopting my rhythms. Cloaking themselves in my words. I worry about it, because I've done it.

Soon after I stopped teaching at Arica to go my own way again, I gave my first major workshop in Texas. I had been so profoundly influenced and impressed by Oscar Ichazo and the Arica Training that I found myself continually saying, "And Oscar says...." or "The Arica approach is...." The first day didn't go that well, and the man who invited me to give the workshops took me aside and said, "Listen, I didn't invite you down here to hear about somebody else's teaching. We want what *you* have to teach." Ironically, I was forced to be free to teach my own way, and the rest of the workshops were necessarily full of spontaneity and improvisation and went wonderfully. That was the critical jolt that catapulted me out of imitation in my teaching from that time on. Since then I've had to incorporate into my own work what I learned from my teachers and forge a fresh, distinctive approach that I could use with complete integrity and authenticity.

Bhagwhan Shree Rajneesh, in one of his early talks, told the following story:

Gurdjieff used to say that you cannot become a man unless you stop being a monkey, and he was right. Somebody asked him: What is the deepest characteristic of a monkey? He said: Copying, imitation. You imitate, you just look around and you follow; in following you become false. You see somebody walking in a certain way, you try to walk that way; somebody is wearing a particular dress, you would like to have that dress. You never look at what your need is. And if you do look to your need, life can become a blissful existence because needs are not much. Imitation will lead you on a path which reaches nowhere in the end. How can you flower if you imitate? You see a musician and you want to be a musician; you see an actor and you want to be an actor. You want to be everything except yourself and that is all that you can be, nothing else.

3. INTUITION

How does it feel
How does it feel
To be on your own
With no direction home
Like a complete unknown
Like a rolling stone?

Bob Dylan[18]

Imitation is, at best, a limited mechanism of self-development, because patterns set by others are not tailor-made for you, and you must move and change to grow. Established ways have rules, traditions, and procedures that tend to stay the same and resist change. And inevitably there comes a time when you have taken what you can from the level of imitation and need to move on. There are various options. You can stay within the path, but make it truly your own and shape it to fit the dynamics of your life. (Thomas Merton remained a Trappist monk for the last twenty-five years of his life, but his writings and activities over that time show an immense amount of change and growth.) Or you can leave one way and adopt another that is more congenial to your particular potential and make that new way distinctively your own. Or you can become disillusioned and acknowledge that you can only go so far in someone else's "length and shadow." At some point, from deep within, we all realize that we're not becoming who we truly want to be and begin to yearn for what we don't have—a rooted connection to an original, creative self.

It is in this longing for more, the tapping of our vital dynamic toward wholeness, that the soul is activated and the shamanic warrior is born. It's through disillusionment—literally, the dispelling of illusion—that we break through to the path of the spirit. You may now continue the journey alone, inspired by the guides you have had in the past and new ones you are sure to meet along the way, or you may come into the company of a teacher who meets you one to one and keeps you moving, without the insulation and restrictions of a fixed method.

It is in disillusionment that you allow yourself to let go. As you surrender to disenchantment, the airtight world that held "the truth" or was "the way," and definitively answered the question "who am I?" vanishes like a childhood fantasy. The experience is devastating and thrilling at the same time. Your world, your reality, your self-image, your identity is disintegrating all around you, yet a whole new world of possibilities is opening up. You're wandering in the dark, and it's both scary and invigorating, intimidating and delicious. You glimpse the possibilities that you have held back or denied in order to imitate someone else. You see you've confined yourself to a procrustean box and now have outgrown it, or wish to. Suddenly, all those repressed feelings, thoughts, and gestures want to break out and dance. You're entering on the perilous passage from unconsciousness and self-consciousness, the realm of personality, to the territory of the soul and spirit. Like Odysseus, you're threatened with being swept into a whirlpool of chaos, never finding your way home to your true self. The threat of falling apart is real. I know ex-Jesuits who go through the rest of their lives disappointed that nothing ever seems as total, as assured, as worthwhile, as all-consuming and admirable as the Jesuit life they could no longer believe in and be satisfied with.

But in each of the shamanic tasks, there's always a point in the middle in which something gets shattered. In the rhythms, staccato yields to chaos, a shattering of form. In feeling, entering into sadness means letting our attachments be shattered. In the life cycles, adolescence and puberty involve shattering bonds with our parents and our upbringing, and breaking out beyond the boundaries of the secure world of childhood. The character work is all about shattering the illusions of the ego.

And so we are at the third level of consciousness which is intuition, and which follows the shattering of the neatly ordered world of imitation and the clearly defined image of one's self. We find ourselves emptied (but also freed) of many structures, beliefs, dogmas, and roles. This happens for some of us in the chaotic freedom of late high school and college. Or after college when the security of being in school, being a student, falls away. Or after leaving the church, an ashram, a dance troupe, a job. It happens in wars (e.g., Vietnam). In divorces. In midlife crises. We encounter the limitations and arbitrariness of all our conditioning.

All this "dismemberment" is necessary for the sort of erasing of personal history that Castaneda and others talk about as vital to awakening the warrior within. All spiritual teachers, all shamans, experience a harrowing initiation in which their life, even their sanity, seems to be shattered. This period of psychic chaos, this dark night of the soul, breaks the grip of conventional reality and propels the teacher, the shaman to a new level. And something like the classic dismemberment that is part of the development of all shamans needs to happen to all of us if we are to break out of the level of imitation to the level of the birth of the spirit.

When I was inspired by La Chunga to give up the dispiriting attempt to dance others' steps and instead gave myself over to freely and passionately expressing myself in my own dancing way, it was a crucial turning point in my development. When my body fell apart so that I could no longer dance, it was another crucial turning point for me. I was then able to discover, in teaching movement to ordinary people, the magic of the five rhythms and the infinitely rich variety of ways people can expressively move. And this movement teaching inevitably led me to discover a new method of improvisational and endlessly varied dancing: Dance of the moment, in the moment, for the moment. And subsequently, I started working with people in a host of ways—whatever ways were freeing, whatever got them moving from inertia toward ecstasy. My progression moved from one-to-one counseling all the way to theater.

At the level of intuition, everything in which you've invested value and power begins to be compromised, to fall apart, and you're left finally with only yourself. A professor once told me that the crucial thing in education is what you know when all the books, all the notes, etc., are taken away. Similarly, when your world falls apart and you're left with just yourself, you're forced to discover who and what you are when you're not fitted out with all the beliefs, the expectations, the views, the self-image provided by some teacher or system.

It's a hard, stormy time. It's painful not only for ourselves but for those around us. And some of us get lost here, caught between the worlds of form and substance, ego and essence, personality and soul. But if you surrender to the chaos of this level of consciousness and let go of the energy that has been stored up so long, you come close to your essential self—the one you buried in the levels of inertia and imitation. Once emptied, you're ready to pay attention to your true self, to listen to and look at the you behind the mask.

This is when the calculating mind gives way to the intuitive mind. Empty of certainty, you search for understanding. Divested of the power of association with some system or teacher or profession, you venture within to find the source of your own power. Now you're open to the messages that come from deep within, the messages no one else in the world receives. And you're free to entertain them, to explore them, to express them, because you're no longer bound by the beliefs, attitudes, habits, dogmas, theories, and prejudices of others. It's no wonder that so many great authors (for example, James Joyce and James Baldwin) have been expatriates, former insiders looking in from outside and framing fresh visions.

Intuition is knowing without thinking. It doesn't involve analysis, comparison, judgment, deduction, or logic. While such calculative thinking is certainly valid and necessary in many areas of our lives, it's vital as well to value and develop our intuition. Intuition is not just a crucial period in our spiritual development, but a critical ingredient in our everyday living.

The simplest way to enhance our intuitive powers is to exercise them. The next time you meet someone new, notice your intuitive, gut feeling about the person the moment you meet. Write it down. Then over the course of your relationship with that person see how accurate your intuition was. We often know instinctively in the gestalt of a first encounter what is true. Our calculating mind eventually comes in later, weighing pros and cons, gathering evidence, etc. Also track your hunches about places, situations, jobs, invitations, and so on. Learn to respect your instincts, your first responses, and give intuition space to operate and develop in your life. It's not only enriching, but ultimately practical. The worst I've ever been ripped off in my life was by someone I mistrusted from the moment I met him. But because I thought I needed him, I allowed that thought to cloud my intuitive, self-protective insight. It's good to let our first instincts develop into feelings and thoughts rather than cutting them short with prejudgments, practical considerations, and so on.

Operating intuitively has become so instinctive with me now that I'm often surprised how unusual it seems to others. Several years ago I was about to address a few hundred business people at a conference, and my husband asked me what I was going to say to this roomful of brilliant and successful people. I said, "I don't know. I have no idea." He responded in shock, "You're crazy. How can you put yourself in that situation?" I had never thought about it and didn't really know what to say, but I responded, "After you jump and before you land is God."

And that's how I feel and move in the world. I jump! It feels scary and edgy sometimes, but it keeps me awake and energized and resourceful.

Once you open up to your intuition, your intuitive flashes engender feelings that cannot be ignored. Once when I was living on the New Jersey coast, I woke up with an overwhelming premonition that something dreadful was going to happen that day. I begged my husband not to go to work and insisted on keeping my son home from school, even though they both thought I was being completely irrational and unreasonable. As the day wore on, the ocean splashed more and more violently against the sea wall until a virtual tidal wave engulfed the town. We ended up first abandoning our townhouse and then our car, walking in blinding snow and knee-deep water to the local soda fountain, while the army and fire department evacuated the town. This sort of intuitive experience has happened so often to me that now I always listen to my instincts and overwhelming feelings.

Intuition has been the lifeblood of my work. I didn't learn it in books or study it with other teachers. In fact, I created my work in reaction to all I'd learned—going against some teachings and recasting the rest in ways that made sense to me. In the beginning, my work was totally spontaneous and in the moment. I made it up as I went along. The only times I felt uncomfortable about this way of doing things was when people asked me what I did for a living. I'd put myself down for not having a ready answer. Still, encouraged by the enthusiastic response of friends and students, I just kept making up exercises to suit the particular people I worked with and the situations I found myself in.

This totally improvisational style might have gone on forever. But one day a young woman declared me her mentor. I said, "I don't want to be your mentor. It's tough enough figuring out things for myself." But she persisted. She wanted me to train her so that she could teach the way I did. Knowing that imitation was a vital first step on the voyage of spiritual self-discovery, I couldn't refuse her heartfelt request.

At first, I just threw her headlong into fresh, challenging situations. But this had only limited value. She legitimately needed to know explicitly what I knew intuitively. And her quest took me to the next level of my own development. She thus was as much my teacher as I was hers. Her needs and her questions stimulated me to make a quantum leap forward. She forced me to discern the central themes of my work, the patterns of my improvising, the truths I operated by, the method in my shamanic madness.

I began to see that I did in fact have a system, however fluid and adaptable, and that many of the exercises, perspectives, and experiments that I created and discarded so whimsically could be perfected and used by others. Thus, the healing powers of creative shamanism could be shared by a widening circle of participants; the teaching wasn't tied to my presence and personality. I learned that I could give away more freely what I'd been given over the years. This new possibility lit up my imagination, and I've spent the last twenty years perfecting this method of shamanic healing. Teaching it. Performing it. Always pushing it into new territory, but building on the solid foundations of convictions tested by long experience. And now I'm writing about it to share the power and the adventure of the dancing path with even more people.

4. IMAGINATION

It is by following the sure lead of your intuitive mind that you find the way from the depths of chaos to the level of imagination. On the other side of falling apart is the process of putting it all together. You return to structure, to system, but now the form is your own creation, a reflection of your distinct identity, experience, vision. The assurance, the originality, the power of great creative artists— whether it be Picasso, Brando, Alice Walker, or Robin Williams—comes from the fact that they've had the courage and the necessity to express what they feel, think, and do, in ways that reflect their own distinct selves. But we are all called upon to be artists of our lives, creating the distinct contribution we alone can make. As much as we admire great artists and performers, we should be inspired by them rather than be in powerless awe of them, the way our TV-watching and star-obsessed society tends to be. Imagine how much of contemporary life is taken up with watching others perform: our society seems consumed by spectator sports, gossipy talk shows and magazines, "Lifestyles of the Rich and Famous," lottery fantasies, and all sorts of other inertial obsessions. Imagination is the level at which you become the star in your own play, getting serious about doing something special with *your* life.

Imagination is the force that pulls your physical, emotional, and mental energies into dynamic harmony, giving wings to your soul. When your imaginative life is rich and generative, you're in vital touch with the rhythms and messages of your body, heart, and mind. You're no longer saying "yes," feeling "no," and acting out "maybe." You're making art of your life, and the radiance of this creative living attracts others who want to live soulfully as well. We all have the capacity for creative integrity, whether we're shoemakers or ballerinas. You just have to determine to settle for nothing less than being fully alive—to show up, be who you are, and share your gifts.

It is at the level of imagination that the warrior self matures. Conceived in imitation and born in intuition, your warrior self now takes charge of your life and you become a dispassionate witness of your own process of development, detaching yourself from the varied forms of its expression, directing the characters you play in the theater of your daily life. You eliminate the tired and predictable characters, and invest more of yourself in those that are vital, enlivening, useful. You identify with the creative archetypes of the self that constitute your dynamic essence—the dancer, singer, poet, actor, healer—and play them out in the many contexts and challenges of your days. Living out of the imagination means more and more moving through fear, anger, and sadness into joy as your basic emotional frequency.

Imagination involves giving your intuitions form. Playing out hunches. Making your visions happen. Enriching your world, putting your mark on it. The way you dress, the way you cook and eat, the way you arrange and furnish your home, the way you speak, write, think, all add up to your personal contribution. And it is your sacred task to express your true self with flare and authenticity, your gift to give the world. When students tell me they'd love to dance like me, I tell them, "Great, then dance like you."

Imagination mobilizes our natural gifts, the things we do naturally and well. For some of us it's business, for others it's teaching, producing, acting, painting, singing, gardening, playing sports, or cooking. It doesn't matter what form your imaginative creativity takes. What matters is that you give expression to your unique gifts and your creative potential, allowing them to manifest in both your inner and outer life. Every day can be special; every day offers the opportunity to enrich your life and the lives of others. Somebody once asked a Huichol Indian why he dressed in his sacred costume every day. He replied in amazement, "Why not? Every day we can be like gods and perform sacred acts."

Our individual destiny is the realization of our unique gifts. Whatever we sincerely yearn to do is what we're meant to be doing. In my experience, when people connect to their creative power and act out of it, the impossible becomes possible and neuroses become irrelevant. Whatever our gifts, it is our responsibility and our privilege to bring them to life. That means doing whatever is necessary—studying, connecting with people, etc. to bring your creativity to fruition. Don't be discouraged by circumstances. As Doris Lessing once said, "Whatever it is you're meant to do, do it now. The conditions are always impossible."

Be generous with your gifts. If you like to write, you don't have to make the bestseller list: write letters to your friends, poems to your lover. Sing to your children. Make something for your mother. Once you enter the creative mode, you discover what it means to live in your soul.

It's important to affirm your power to visualize your heart's desires and thereby make them happen. Many years ago I reached a crisis point in my relationships with men. I'd had three negative experiences in a row. I told my best friend that that was it. I was giving up on men. She laughed and said, "Gabrielle, what is it that you want? Describe your dream man to me." I thought she was just kidding. But she was serious, so I stopped and thought about it for the first time. At first I said, "I don't have a dream man." But as soon as I said that, I knew it wasn't true. And I realized that if I wanted a real lasting, loving relationship in my life, then the first step was to acknowledge it. So I just let myself say exactly what I wanted: "I want a tall, Jewish lawyer with kids who lives in the East and is very happy with himself and his work. I want him to be deeply spiritual and charged with his own creative power." Then I visualized this person coming into my life: a tall, thin man with a briefcase. Three days later, I met Robert. We've been together ever since. I had simply stopped the world for a moment and had given wholehearted thought to what I truly wanted and put some energy into creating it for myself. I also gave myself permission to have what I wanted.

I've also used my imagination to heal others. I once went to visit a Hopi rattle maker in Arizona. It took all of my intuitive powers to find her house high up in the mountains, having to make choices of which way to go every hundred feet or so. When I arrived, her granddaughter was crying in pain, holding her ears. She had had a terrible earache for twenty-four hours. Instinctively, I approached the five-year-old and told her, "I'm going to put my hand on your ear and take away the pain. I want you to see the pain. What does it look like? What shape is it? What color? What does it sound like? Does it smell? How would it feel if you touched it? Now I want you to imagine it leaving your ear and entering my hand." She looked up at me with huge brown eyes full of trust. I put my hand on her ear, held it there a few minutes, and then ran to the door and blew the pain out of my hand and closed the door. Within seconds the pain was gone. Her grandmother, the rattle maker, stood there grinning from ear to ear. "That's what my grandfather would have done," she said. "He was a shaman."

In a few minutes, the room seemed to fill with people. Someone placed a chair in the middle of the room and people took turns sitting in it, asking for a healing. Headaches, sores, back pains, and so on. In each case I trusted myself to do what came naturally. It's a day I'll never forget, as I discovered the range of my healing powers as they were drawn out by people for whom healing power was natural medicine.

Imagination is powerful. Imagination is healing. All you need is the courage to visualize what should be, and then give yourself to its creation. The result may not be what you expected, but it will be right.

5. INSPIRATION

Inspiration is the level at which conscious creation ceases. Philosophers tell of thoughts coming from nowhere. Writers find themselves instruments of a voice speaking through them. Artists speak of themselves as mediums for visions. Athletes look with amazement at tapes of feats they've achieved and have no idea how they did them. I know that in dance there are times when I'm beyond self-consciousness, even consciousness, and simply merge with the music, the motion. There's only dancing.

It's possible to infuse your living more and more with this art beyond art, beyond boundaries, definitions, intentions, regrets. Pure energy, constant dance, totally connected to the life force that vibrates through you. When we experience moments of ecstasy—in play, in stillness, in art, in sex—they come not as an exception, an accident, but as a taste of what life is meant to be. Why shouldn't we be able to live more and more in ecstasy, if we have the courage to venture out of inertia and imitation into intuition and imagination? Ecstasy is an ideal, a goal, but it can be the expectation of every day. Those times when we're grounded in our body, pure in our heart, clear in our mind, rooted in our soul, and suffused with the energy, the spirit of life, are our birthright. It's really not that hard to stop and luxuriate in the joy and wonder of being. Children do it all the time. It's a natural human gift that should be at the heart of our lives. Like Arjuna in the *Bhagavad Gita*, our warrior call is to be still, at perfect peace in the midst of battle, at essence no warrior at all. In our deepest center we are, as T.S. Eliot put it, "the stillpoint of the turning world," the rhythm beyond stillness, the feeling beyond compassion, the life force beyond death, the level deeper than inspiration itself. The moving center.

At the level of inspiration you enrich life with your own rituals. You connect naturally with the great myths and symbols. Ritual and myth seem your natural language. Your wishes take on the character of prayer. Like the Huichol Indians, every day is a sacred occasion. And as Starhawk, author of *The Spiral Dance*, says, "Ritual and myth are like seed crystals of new patterns that can eventually reshape the culture around them." Your wishes, because they are pure, can bring things into being and connect you with the way the universe is moving.

At this level you realize that no one can organize your perception of God better than you can. Your own sense of ritual and theater can mark every day, as well as special occasions, with the celebration of spirit. Ritual infuses your life, but the liturgy comes from within. Your body prays in its own ways, your altar is a moveable feast of images and settings. In meditation, moving or still, you listen to your center, the stillpoint of your turning world, receiving illuminations, overarching insights, glimpses of ultimate unity. You are a wave of energy, a partner in the cosmic dance, a spark of the consuming fire that lights and moves all things, surrendered to the force of life pulsing through you. You are caught up in ecstasy.

I find myself more and more drawn to solitude and silence. I can be alone for hours, days, or weeks, and bask in the luxury of my being. I can commune with myself, ask questions and wait for answers. I pray for direction, and the universe sends me visions. Silence is the sister of solitude. Practice not speaking for a few hours a day. The monks know something about coming to your self. Practicing silence for a day once a week is a great inspiration to self-observation, to centering and cultivating your distinct perspective. Solitude and silence are invitations to our deepest self.

The dancing path to ecstasy is a spiral with no beginning or end. The movement from inertia through imitation, intuition, imagination, and inspiration to ecstasy is the neverending, ever-changing dance of life. In inertia our fullness is empty; in ecstasy our emptiness is full.

I have devoted more than twenty years of my life to the art of healing and the healing power of art. The next turn in the road for me as a teacher is to train others to teach my version of western Zen. Eastern Zen is sitting. Western Zen is moving. I am a devotee of a dancing god, the invisible spirit that animates all the great traditions of myth and religion. And everyone must dance the dance distinctively for themselves with body, heart, mind, soul, and spirit. Anything else is idol worship, and no road to ecstasy.

6. WAYS TO THE CENTER

Relaxation is a key to the awakening of intuition, imagination, and the flow of inspiration in our lives. Here's a version of the simple relaxation I used with my father when he was dying, and with hundreds of other people:

Lie down on the floor. Feel the weight of your body sinking into the floor. Surrender to its drift. Feel your breath rising and sinking, expanding and contracting in your body. Listen to your heart beat.

Now imagine a wave of warm, peaceful energy coming in your toes and relaxing all the tiny muscles and tendons in your feet ... feel this energy encircling your ankles and moving into your calves.... Your feet and calves feel warm and heavy, as if baked in a hot desert sun ... let this warm, heavy energy move up your legs and into your pelvis ... let it open to receive this slow flow of honeyed energy.... Feel your muscles and organs all relaxing as this energy flows up your spine, vertebra by vertebra, into your solar plexus and from there into your chest, and shoulders, down your arms and into your hands, relaxing every inch of your body.... Your whole body feels warm, heavy, as this energy moves into your neck and head, relaxing all the muscles and tendons. Feel the warm energy wash over your face, let your eyes sink into your head, your cheekbones relax, your jaw drop ... your whole being is suffused with this penetrating bath of warm energy.... Ride the wave of your breath like a surfer into the depths of yourself, in and out, deeper and deeper, rising and sinking, expanding and contracting, feeling the movements of life, the infusion of spirit ... you're being breathed from the top of your head to the tips of your toes ... your whole body is now filled with the spirit of life.

Another exercise you can do is to visualize your spirit animal. It is a virtual universal in shamanic healing to summon a spirit animal to guide you on your way and keep you in touch with your true nature. The spiritual connection between human beings and animals goes back to the earliest days of human evolution, although most of us have completely lost any sense, apart from team mascots and cartoons, of our vital connection to the animal world of which we are actually an integral part. Our spirit animal connects us deeply to the earth while guiding us in the land of the spirit. I have three spirit animals—the silver wolf, the raven, and the dolphin. The silver wolf and raven are my personal guides; the dolphin guides my work.

Your spirit animal may not be your favorite animal, or even one that you have any contact with. But it is the one that has the lessons you need to learn and will in some way reflect a part of your nature. Usually when someone tells me their spirit animal I feel an immediate shock of recognition, "Aha! Of course." One of my friends is an owl. And she truly is one: she comes awake at night and even looks a bit like an owl.

Here's a way to contact your spirit animal:

First do a deep relaxation exercise. The simplest is to lie on the floor with your eyes closed and listen to soothing, trance-like music, like side one of my tape *Totem*. Feel the music entering your body, your chest, your shoulders, your arms, your hands, your neck, your face, your hair, and then feel it in your belly. When the music ends, let it go and count down from ten to zero.

At zero imagine yourself in a beautiful natural setting—high in the mountains or on the beach or in a forest; by a lake or in a desert—let the scene come to you naturally, don't impose it. In this beautiful place, find a comfortable spot and sit and wait. Listen for a melody. You may hear it in the wind, or in the waves, or in the silence. Pick up on it and sing or hum it. Use it to call your spirit animal. After you've been singing for a while with your whole heart and spirit, body and soul, let it go. Within a few minutes your spirit animal will appear. Receive this animal with love. Ask it what teaching it brings to you today. Accept any feelings or thoughts that come to you. When it seems time, let it go. But know that whenever you need it you need only hum or sing or hear within you the melody, and the animal will return to guide and instruct. For now, let it go by taking a few deep breaths, slowly counting zero to ten, and on ten open your eyes.

A way of quickly getting to the level of inspiration at almost any time once you've worked through this book thoroughly, is to put all the dimensions of shamanic healing through the rhythms. I regularly use the rhythms to get grounded and centered and to arrive at the stillpoint from which authentic, healing action flows. Here's one of the countless ways to do it:

Listen to your heart beat. Feel your breath moving deep in your center. Begin a *flowing*, repetitive movement. Let it grow bigger and bigger. Surrender more and more of yourself to this movement. Add sound. Let the sound move deeper and deeper until the sound and movement merge into one dynamic harmony. Feel the specific shape, the contour of your movement. Visualize it as an image, a visual energy, and then transpose this image onto paper with a pencil, pen, crayon, paintbrush.

Then do this with the *staccato, chaos, lyric,* and *stillness* rhythms, turning each into a visualization that springs from movement and sound.

Then put each drawing into words. Sit and wait for the words to come: contemplate your drawing and let it speak to you. A flowing poem. A staccato poem. A chaos poem. A lyric poem. A stillness poem.

Now blend the movement, sound, and poetry together in the midst of your drawings. Create your own little theater piece—moving, singing, and speaking your vision.

You've transformed yourself into a holy actor.

Still another exercise that I use in many of my workshops to heal our relationships to ourselves is the body drawing. Here's how to do it:

Get a piece of butcher paper, long and wide enough for your whole body to be drawn on it. Lie down on your back on the paper and have someone trace your outline.

Look at your shape. What statement does it make? What's going on? Write it down somewhere outside the perimeters of the body drawing. Look inside the shape. What's going on? Just sit and breathe and look and feel your energy. Using crayons, markers, paintbrushes, etc., fill in the body with the energy you feel. Sit back again. What is your inner rhythm, your basic pulse? What does it feel like to be you? Let this feeling flow from your center through your arm into your hand and out your drawing instrument onto the paper. Sit back once again. Contemplate your body, your energy, in the visualization in front of you. Where does your fear live in your body? (When I looked at my body outline, I saw how stiff and elevated my shoulders were and instantly I knew where I held my fear, how I lived in a constant state of alert.) Where's your anger? Your sadness? Put them into your drawing. Where is your joy? Your compassion?

Where is your mother in your body? Your father? How do they live on in your body? (My mother lives in my mouth and my feet. I feel her in my arms when I reach out to hold someone. And in my stomach when I can't quite digest something.) Get in touch with feeling memories and put them into the drawing.

What does your shape tell you about how you feel about yourself? Give your shape a voice and write a few lines from its perspective on the side of your drawing somewhere near your head. Fill in your heart. What if your heart could speak? What line would it say? Write it to the left of your trunk. What do your hands want to do? Your muscles? Your skin? Your pores? Let them speak to you. Just sit and gaze at this image of yourself. Then, move on impulse and pour yourself out onto the paper, filling in as much as you can, until there's nothing left but your breath, moving in and out, rising and falling, looking in the mirror of itself.

Once your intuition and imagination are awakened and exercised, once you begin to experience inspiration, you'll invent all sorts of ways to discover and catalyze your energy.

7. HEALING

Ultimately shamanic healing means working with the spirit. Regardless of clothing, ritual, tools, or tradition, the shaman is a spirit worker. It is the only kind of healing that I'm capable of. When people ask me what sort of healing I do, I tell them: If you've broken your leg, go see a doctor. But if you're living in your head split off from your body, if your feelings are choked up, if your mind is good at everything except what really matters, if you've lost your soul, if your life lacks spirit, then seek out a shaman. Or better yet, discover your shamanic powers within.

By now you're aware of not only your potential but also your current weaknesses and limitations. Yet every shaman is a wounded healer. Those who have everything, the perfectly content, never move out of inertia. No wonder Jesus said that it was harder for a rich man to enter the kingdom of heaven than for a camel to pass through the eye of a needle. Knowing your poverty, your neediness, is vital to movement on the dancing path. The devastating wounds of anorexia in my youth and then being unable to dance later on were vital to my development. And my wounds give me sympathy for what others are going through and remind me how they can find wholeness through adversity.

We all share the wound of fragmentation. And we can all share in the cure of unification. Healing is the unification of all our forces—the powers of being, feeling, knowing, and seeing.

I look in the mirror and I look out the window and I see myself and others struggling to be in our bodies. Struggling to know who we are and what we need. To like ourselves, rather than wanting to be somebody else, or somewhere else. I see our inability to relate, to communicate from the heart, to overcome our distance and alienation from one another, avoiding each other's eyes, at a loss to know what others need. I see people searching for direction, trying to summon up their personal power, longing for the strength to be independent.

The wounded healer in me knows that healing our driven selves comes from our ability to empower our bodies, hearts, minds, souls, and spirits once more, bringing them into vital unity. Spiritual healing means taking responsibility for being a whole person. We have to take responsibility for being a body, for having a heart, for possessing a mind, for awakening our soul, for opening to our spirit. We need to do right by our body, purify our relationships, use our mind for creative freedom and not enslavement, free the soul from the ego, and undertake the spiritual journey. A whole person is an inspired person, one who embodies the spirit.

Disease is inertia. Healing is movement. Shamanic work is about dancing from within. If you put the body in motion, you will change. You are meant to move: from flowing to staccato, through chaos into lyric and back into the stillness from which all movement comes.

If you let your heart be moved, be open to the risk and the adventure of feelings, letting them work through to completion, you will change. Tears turn into smiles, anger into embraces.

If you free your mind to experience and complete each of your life cycles, integrating their teachings and tasks, you will change. It's when you stop moving through life that you get caught out of place, that you react to adult situations with childhood emotions. Moving completely through life makes you whole.

If you awaken your soul, you will change. Engage your characters. Watch yourself act them out. Master them, and you're free to be, feel, think, and act as your distinct self.

The spirit in motion heals, expands, circles in and out of the body, moving us through the layers of consciousness from inertia to ecstasy. Open to the spirit, and you will be transformed.

Movement is my medium and my metaphor. I know that if a wave of energy is allowed to complete itself it yields a whole new wave, and in fact, that is all I really know. Riding these waves means joining the cosmic dance of love that, as Dante says, "moves the sun and the other stars."

EPILOGUE

At the stillpoint of the turning world
there the dance is.
And without the point
that stillpoint
there would be no dance
and there is only the dance.

T.S. Eliot[19]

My life has been a search for the stillpoint, the Silver Desert, the place of true healing. I have sought to awaken and nourish my sacred instincts and encourage you to do the same. This is not mere selfishness, but a means to change, for ourselves and our world. Unconsciousness is a disease that affects our planet.

Imagine the self-destructive possibilities when there is no maternal instinct functioning in a collective—whether it be a family, society, or the world—where people treat the earth body collectively with as little respect as they do their own, individually. Imagine the alienation when there is no paternal instinct operating in a collective, when people relate solely at the surface and cannot see each other's true needs and gifts—a whole nation of people chanting "me first." Imagine the conformity and repression in a society with no internal instinct; the disharmony and war when there is no fraternal instinct; the materialism and lack of spiritual values when there is no eternal instinct.

Does it sound familiar? What can be done about it? What do you have the power to change? Only yourself, really, and the evolution of your consciousness is a fundamental part of the hologram of existence, of the unity of all things, of our indivisible reality.

Movement is the medium of change. In my experience, if you put your psyche in motion it will heal itself. The enemy is inertia, be it of energy in the body, walls around the heart, or fixed attitudes in the mind. Movement is the medicine.

The maps I've given you are only guides for your journey through the territory of your psyche; they aren't the territory itself. They have no value other than as an aid to you as you travel through the mysteries of an ever-changing self. The shamanic journey is yours to take. It won't look like mine or anyone else's. And, if you don't take your journey, no one will.

Each of us has the power and responsibility to heal ourselves, to be our own medicine man or woman. Awakening our innate shamanic powers of being, loving, knowing, seeing, and healing involves ongoing work at all levels and in all dimensions of our self. Exploring the range of rhythms and emotions, achieving insights into our conditioning and ego, moving through the energy levels of the spirit—these are all activities to be integrated into our daily lives.

When you work with the maps in this book, explore the way they overlap and connect. The more I work with them, the deeper they take me into the threads of the psyche. I'm interested in inertia and I'm interested in fear, but I'm much more interested in the connection between them— how fear breeds inertia, or how sadness relates to puberty, or how lack of mother equals fear, or how lyrical is joy.

The road to the self is not a straight line. It's a continuum of circles, cycles, and waves that are all interconnected. Rhythms are connected to feelings are connected to sexual waves are connected to the life cycles are connected to archetypes are connected to levels of consciousness. Being is connected to birth is connected to mother is connected to body is connected to fear is connected to inertia is connected to the flow. So, too, with death, the universe, spirit, stillness, compassion, inspiration, celibacy, and healing.

All these energies come together in you. In your deepest center, you are the stillpoint. You are the rhythm beyond stillness, the feeling beyond compassion, the sexual energy beyond celibacy, the life-force beyond death, the vibration beyond inspiration.

You are the moving center.

Gabrielle Roth

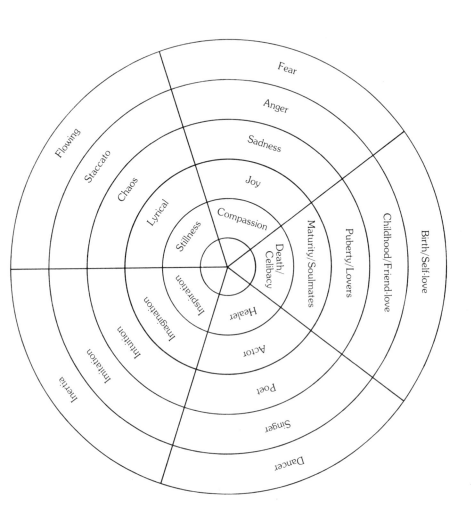

NOTES

1. Joan Halifax, *Shaman: The Wounded Healer*, New York: Crossroad, 1982, p. 66.

2. From *Pray Body*, © 1986 by Gabrielle Roth.

3. Patti Smith, "Ain't it Strange," *Babel*, New York: G.P. Putnam's, 1978, p. 69. Reprinted by permission of the Putnam Publishing Group from BABEL by Patti Smith. Copyright © 1978 by Patti Smith.

4. Peter Gabriel, "The Rhythm of the Heat," *Security*, Geffen Records, 1982.

5. Jelaluddin Rumi, *The Ruins of the Heart*, trans. Edmund Helminski, Putney, Vt.: Threshold Books, 1981, pp. 31-32.

6. I saw this quotation in an art exhibit.

7. Erich Fromm, *The Sane Society*, New York: W.W. Norton, 1955, p. 3.

8. Robert Frost, from interview in George Plimpton (ed.), *Writers at Work: Second Series*, New York: Viking, 1963.

9. Sam Shepard, "The Tooth of the Crime," *Sam Shepard: Seven Plays*, New York: Bantam, 1981, p. 227.

10. Carlos Castaneda, *A Separate Reality*, New York: Pocket, 1972, p. 90.

11. Quoted in the *New York Times*, Dec. 15, 1987.

12. Carlos Castaneda, *The Fire From Within*, New York: Simon and Schuster, 1984, p. 28.

13. All theater material from *Mirrors*, copyright © 1981-1987 by Gabrielle Roth.

14. Carl Jung, quoted in Richard Kehl, *Silver Departures*, La Jolla: Green Tiger Press, 1983, p.56.

15. Carlos Castaneda, *The Fire From Within*, p. 37.

16. Mircea Eliade, *Shamanism: Archaic Techniques of Ecstasy*, Princeton, N.J.: Princeton Univ. Press, 1964, p. 4.

17. From the title of Doris Lessing's recent book *Prisons We Choose to Live Inside*, New York: Harper & Row, 1988.

18. Bob Dylan, "Like a Rolling Stone," © 1965 WARNER BROS. INC. All rights reserved. Used by permission.

19. From "Burnt Norton," in *Four Quartets*, by T.S. Eliot. Copyright 1943 by T.S. Eliot; © 1971 renewed by Esme Valerie Eliot. Reprinted by permission of Harcourt Brace Jovanovich, Inc.

ABOUT THE AUTHOR

Gabrielle Roth has taught her unique style of shamanic healing throughout the United States, Canada, and Europe. She has produced concerts and public radio programs, created numerous music and speaking tapes, and has acted as consultant to various educational institutions, mental hospitals, and professional associations. Gabrielle has worked with her own dance/theater/music company, the "Mirrors," has been a member of the Actor's Studio (Playwrights and Directors Unit) and has directed Off-Off-Broadway and experimental plays.

She is currently teaching experimental theater in New York and is training others to use her shamanic methods in various artistic, educational, and healing contexts.

Gabrielle's life has been devoted to empowering people through the creative process, inspiring them to free themselves, to transform their daily lives into sacred art. In this book, she makes available to the general public what she's discovered—the ways to come fully alive.

For further information concerning the work of Gabrielle Roth, please write or call:

THE MOVING CENTER
P.O. Box 2034
Red Bank, New Jersey 07701
1-800-76-RAVEN

Nataraj Publishing

is committed to acting as a catalyst for change and transformation in the world by providing books and tapes on the leading edge in the fields of personal and social consciousness growth. "Nataraj" is a Sanskrit word referring to the creative, transformative power of the universe. For more information on our company, please contact us at:

Nataraj Publishing
1561 South Novato Blvd.
Phone: (415) 899-9666
Fax: (415) 899-9667

Music by Gabrielle Roth & The Mirrors
Cassettes $9.95 / CDs $14.95

Tongues. An inspirational and celebratory album filled with rich, exotic textures over a funky, driving beat.

Luna. Nominated for an INDIE as Best New Age Album of 1994. This music weaves a sensuous web of mystery and delight as it echoes deep into our ancestral bones and celebrates the dawn and dusk of our humanity.

*Trance.** Music that calls the soul into the body, the body into the beat, and the beat into your belly.

Ritual. Trance music for movement, meditation, massage and other rituals.

Waves. An ecstatic whirlpool of rhythm and voice.

*Bones.** A calling to the inner dance, the dance around your bones.

*Initiation.** A musical map from inertia to ecstasy.

Totem. The underground classic, an urban-primitive dance experience.

*Contains the Five Rhythms

Videos by Gabrielle Roth

The Wave: Ecstatic Dance for Body and Soul. Gabrielle's revolutionary moving meditation which illustrates the rhythm work described in this book. ($24.95)

I Dance the Body Electric. Gabrielle in warm and spirited conversation about her unique approach to healing through the creative process and living life as art. ($19.95)

To Place an Order
Call 1-800-949-1091.

Other Books and Tapes from Nataraj Publishing

Books

Living in the Light: A Guide to Personal and Planetary Transformation. By Shakti Gawain with Laurel King. The recognized classic on developing intuition and using it as a guide in living your life. (Trade paperback $11.95)

Return to the Garden: A Journey of Discovery. By Shakti Gawain. Shakti reveals her path to self-discovery and personal power and shows us how to return to our personal garden and live on earth in a natural and balanced way. (Trade paperback $9.95)

Awakening: A Daily Guide to Conscious Living. By Shakti Gawain. A daily meditation guide that focuses on maintaining your spiritual center not just when you are in solitude, but when you are in the world, and especially, in relationships. (Trade paperback $9.95)

Awakening the Warrior Within: Secrets of Personal Safety and Inner Security. By Dawn Callan. This book explodes contemporary myths about attaining personal safety, revealing how they may actually contribute to our victimization, and introduces the Warrior Code—ten important keys for making the journey back to power. (Trade paperback $12.95)

Embracing Our Selves: The Voice Dialogue Manual. By Drs. Hal and Sidra Stone. The highly acclaimed, groundbreaking work that explains the psychology of the selves and the Voice Dialogue method. (Trade paperback $12.95)

Coming Home: The Return to True Self. By Martia Nelson. A down-to-earth spiritual primer that explains how we can use the very flaws of our humanness to carry the vibrant energy of our true self and reach the potential that dwells in all of us. (Trade paperback $12.95)

The Path of Transformation: How Healing Ourselves Can Change the World. By Shakti Gawain. Shakti gave us *Creative Visualization* in the 70s, *Living in the Light* in the 80s, and now *The Path of Transformation* for the 90s. Shakti's new bestseller delivers an inspiring and provocative message for the path of true transformation. (Trade paperback $9.95)

The Revelation: A Message of Hope for the New Millennium. By Barbara Marx Hubbard. An underground classic from one of the true prophets of our time. Hubbard offers an astonishing interpretation of the Book of Revelation, which reveals the consciousness required by the human race, not only to survive, but to blossom into full realization of its potentials. (Trade paperback $16.95)

What Women and Men Really Want: Creating Deeper Understanding and Love in Our Relationships. By Aaron Kipnis and Elizabeth Herron. Two of America's most popular experts on relationships take a group of women and men into the wilderness for a week to explore gender conflicts. Against the backdrop of nature, the women and men bare their hearts on many highly charged issues, yielding a fresh new vision of how we can all enjoy more whole and fulfilling relationships. (Trade paperback $12.95)

Write from the Heart: Unleashing the Power of Your Creativity. By Hal Zina Bennett. The author of more than 25 successful books unveils the secrets of good writing. Bennett teaches how to draw from the deep creative source that is the wellspring of every successful writer's craft. A special chapter maps out the world of publishing to guide you through the steps for getting your work published. (Trade paperback $11.95)

Tapes

Living in the Light: Read by Shakti Gawain. Shakti reads her bestseller. (Two cassettes $15.95)

Developing Intuition. Shakti Gawain expands on the ideas about intuition she first discussed in *Living in the Light.* (One cassette $10.95)

The Path of Transformation: How Healing Ourselves Can Change the World. Shakti reads her inspiring new bestseller. (Two 70-minute cassettes $15.95)

To Place an Order

Call 1-800-949-1091.